THE NEW HEALTHCARE LEADER'S GUIDE

(2025 Edition)

For those **in pursuit of excellence** in a crazy complex industry

For Clinical & Nonclinical Leaders

LORI A MALLORY, MHSA, FACMPE

ISBN: 979-8-89694-623-6 - eBook
ISBN: 979-8-89694-624-3 - Paperback
ISBN: 979-8-89694-625-0 - Hardcover

Dedicated to my first grandson, Baker James Mallory,
who was also born in 2025 along with this book.
May your journey be filled with purpose and a heart that inspires kindness wherever you go!

And to the future healthcare leaders,
May your passion and dedication transform lives and elevate humanity.

Contents

"I've learned that people will forget what you said, people will forget what you did, but people will never forget how you made them feel."

—Maya Angelou

Part I

What's Happening Today

The intent of this section is to not only level set on why this book is essential for new leaders, but to also provide a broader lens on what is happening across the healthcare ecosystem. Today's healthcare leader has elevated responsibilities that require a scope redefinition of exactly what is involved in the profession. When you first launch your career, you know only one small sliver of the big picture. Use this to spark your imagination!

“The healthcare industry is undergoing seismic shifts that are redefining care delivery, payment models, and market dynamics...”

—Advisory Board, 2024[1]

1 This is an understatement!

Chapter 1

In Pursuit of Excellence

"Excellence is the next five minutes ... or not."

—Tom Peters[2]

The Backstory

Healthcare has been my career now for over 25 years. I often wonder exactly how this happened. So much has changed, and yet it seems so little true progress has been made. I started in the space right after my boys were born and after an exhilarating post-college career in telecommunication sales and sales leadership. Despite the success there, I had always wanted to be a physician and even had a $50 bet with an elementary school teacher that I would do just that. *(Yes, I've tried to find him, to give him the money, but I can't seem to find him.... If anyone knows a Mr. Woods from Grandview, Missouri circa 1978, please let me know).*

My upbringing didn't exactly provide me with a cheerleading squad that encouraged academic achievement, nor do I think

2 Calling all leaders focused on people: read all things Tom!

any meaningful family member even asked what my goals might be. Miraculously I followed my sister to what was then Central Missouri State University, its name now much more dignifying, The University of Central Missouri (Go Mules!). I had a wonderful experience and did receive a solid education… but alas, no medical school. Fast forward to six years post undergrad, and I found that my mind wouldn't leave the idea alone. I knew one thing: that the next step was to learn more about this dream of mine. I ended up following a dear friend and ob/gyn physician around as she did procedures at an area hospital. Yikes! I blacked out within moments of watching a colposcopy procedure, and as I literally slid out the room and down the wall in the hall, I thanked God that I seemed to have skills in leadership.

My friend and I connected after that memorable morning for lunch, and she was sharing with me what a disaster the business of medicine was for many practices across the country. A series of complex issues, ranging from basic office lease agreements to malpractice insurance to staffing and health plan reimbursement, had made it so physician leaders were grappling with how to run a strong business and practice medicine. It was a lot, and at that time, technology wasn't even really in the picture and strong degree programs in healthcare administration were rare and primarily served hospital administrators. Most office leaders were a family member of the lead physician and likely had no more skills in the space than they could learn around the dinner table. I was intrigued and offered to do an operational assessment of her practice for free as a learning for myself. She graciously agreed, and while there are a lot of fun details about what happened next, in short, the rest is history. I left a job at a

Fortune 500 company where I was on the Vice President track at the young age of 28 and took the leap into healthcare leadership.

It's been a great joy in my life. I hope what I share of my experience in this book will help spark or continue to ignite your excitement for this incredibly important profession.

The Then and Now and Why the Chapter Title

The reason I called this chapter "In Pursuit of Excellence" is not because of the book of the same name. My call to healthcare was to help our nation, and perhaps our world, have a better healthcare system. Isn't that what the strong majority, clinical or not, hopes for? To make a difference in the lives of those around us and to advance the health and communities of those we serve. If that's not your goal and if you don't feel "called" to this sector, I would highly recommend you consider exploring what truly sets your heart on fire. **This profession requires both an incredible passion and a deep inner desire to continuously learn and take action in a highly complex and constantly changing ecosystem.** When you step into healthcare leadership, you will be a student for a lifetime—and to me, that's awesome![3]

I was new to the profession when the Malcolm Baldridge National Quality Award was established by the US Congress. It gave its first healthcare sector award in 1999 to Sutter Davis Hospital in California. That propelled me to become a student of qualitative and quantitative excellence. I wanted to be the best in my field, and to do that meant to understand just

3 (In Pursuit of Excellence, How to win in sport and life through mental training, Terry Orlick, PhD (Sports psychologist) , originally published in 1980)

what that meant—at least on paper and from an objective perspective at that point in time. The Baldridge Award 5 "Ps" framework (below) started to help shape my understanding of what needed to be considered to pursue excellence. The achievement categories were broad, and the ideas just flat out resonated with what I thought it would take to truly be exceptional across a large industry such as healthcare. Their framework allowed me to begin to distill my thinking on what is truly important.

Malcolm Baldridge National Quality Awards Areas of Assessment

1. **Purpose:** The organization's mission, vision and values that guide its goals and strategies.
2. **People** (my favorite part): The employees, leadership and stakeholders involved in the organization.
3. **Processes:** The methods and procedures used to achieve the organization's objectives and deliver products and services.
4. **Products:** The goods and services provided by the organization.
5. **Performance:** The outcomes and results achieved by the organization, including customer satisfaction, financial performance and overall effectiveness.

Frameworks such as this are even more important now than ever. The flood of information we have ready access to creates the need to employ focus as one of the most important skills you will need as you embark on greatness in your field.

The reason for this book is to help our country experience exceptional and sustainable healthcare for all people. It is also rooted in my concern that our academic programs need additional support as they prepare tomorrow's leaders. Let me give you an example.

As a healthcare executive now for many years, I have had the opportunity to interview many recent graduates of healthcare administration programs from multiple states. I have also had the opportunity to work with many exceptional physicians, advanced practice practitioners (nurse practitioners/physician assistants) and nurses who find themselves in a position where the profession desperately needs and wants them to serve in leadership positions as well as practice medicine.

I have a few go-to interview questions, but I like to begin with what I consider a warm-up question — for example, 'Can you tell me about Value-Based Care?' I have been stunned that frankly more than 80 percent cannot answer that basic question in a way that makes sense within the context of how it is actually used on the front lines in the healthcare system today. I then go on to another basic question: "Who is doing something exciting in the healthcare space?"

Again, beyond some expected tech answers, the majority don't know what is going on across our country. So, within moments, I would find myself doubtful that our team could find a healthcare leader who could truly jump in and help our team quickly. With this in mind, I learned to lean into a personal belief I've always held, which is somewhat of a famous saying: "Where there is a frustration, there is an opportunity."

So, here I sit today, one month into a year-long sabbatical, and hoping to make even a small dent in what I feel is a significant need for our nation's healthcare system. We need prepared and strong leaders, and we need a lot of them across so many diverse categories that make up our healthcare system. It is important, it is exciting, and my friends, we are now **in pursuit of excellence in healthcare leadership education.** I'm so glad you are here!

What You Can Expect

In this book, I want to commit to you a few things:

1. I am going to keep the thoughts high level. No one needs a tome to dig through. This book is meant to be a handbook that can offer some key learnings for new healthcare leaders. Alas, as complex as the industry is there is simply no way to include all aspects. *(Even as I've worked thru the final steps to get this book out into the world, I think of something almost daily that could have been included.)*
2. I am going to provide short real-world examples throughout the book so that you can be sure to walk away with what is currently happening in the healthcare ecosystem. My goal is that they help bring to life the concepts discussed.
3. I will summarize each chapter with 3 big ideas from the chapter—what I call The Big 3. As I shared, the intent here is to cover the basics. That said, I want to be here for you. Please always feel free to reach out via LinkedIn. I will do my best to help you in any way I can as you advance your knowledge and embark on a career in this wonderful profession.

As far as structure, I am all in on the number 13... It's been my favorite number way before Taylor Swift claimed it. We will have 13 total chapters, including this one, which you are now done with, so yay for that.

In the book, there are three sections or parts.

I. What's Happening Today: This section focuses on the most important subject areas that you should have a strong command of as a healthcare leader. It will also highlight the many facets of healthcare (like hospitals, payers, pharmacy) and who is doing something special and exciting within those spaces. This section is designed to get you excited about your career ahead!

II. Mini "Masterclasses": Here is where I am going to dive into core topics. **I will spend quite a bit of time talking about the Team/aka the people and the culture you grow as a leader. (In my opinion, this is the most important lesson for an aspiring leader, which is why I picked Tom Peters for the quote above. He's the guru writer on all things PEOPLE FIRST.)** I will also cover the traditional topics, which include Payers, Providers, Payer/Provider partnerships, and Value-Based Care (VBC)

III. Future Scan: I will discuss where healthcare is going, and the leadership principles needed to ensure we are moving toward excellence.

The Big 3 (In Summary)

- **This profession requires both an incredible passion and a deep inner desire to continuously learn and take action in a highly complex and constantly changing ecosystem.**
- **Excellence comes down to strong frameworks, such as the Malcolm Baldridge Award criteria, which helps leaders think clearly about complex processes and problems by breaking them down into clear focus areas. (In this example, it was Purpose, People, Processes, Products and Performance.)**
- **As the healthcare industry evolves, healthcare leadership education is more important now than ever. It's important to stay informed—and stay excited about what we can achieve.**

So, let's get to it and see what's happening on the ground.

"Positive attention. . . is thirty times more powerful than negative attention in creating high performance on a team. . . . People don't need feedback. They need attention, and, moreover, attention to what they do the best. And they become more engaged and therefore more productive when we give it to them."

—Marcus Buckingham and Ashley Goodall

Chapter 2

Today's Healthcare Ecosystem

"True transformation in healthcare requires visionary leaders who are willing to challenge the status quo, reimagine systems, and inspire others to act in ways that prioritize patient outcomes over tradition."

—Dr. Toby Cosgrove, former CEO of the Cleveland Clinic

The Playing Field

I want to start with the three major players to make sure we level set first on who is almost in every conversation!

1. **The patient themselves.** "Health is wealth" is now a common saying. If you or a family member have ever been sick, you know this well. There is nothing you can do whether rich or poor if you don't have your health. **The patient is *the* key party and our constant focus.** They have a personal investment in becoming a part of the healthcare system: to get healthier

(whether it be through conventional or holistic medicine), ensure future health (by participating in preventive medicine), and to remedy specific, perhaps even persistent, medical issues (whether chronic or acute conditions).

2. **The providers of care.** The main purveyors of healthcare include "wellness companies" (physical fitness, chiropractic care, acupuncture, massage, yoga, fitness, mindfulness, supplements, etc.), "primary care providers" (pediatrics, family practice, internal medicine) and then of course there are those designated for what I will refer to as "sick and repair providers." These include your basic urgent care, primary care practices (Actually the best place for basic sick/repair care), specialists by condition, skilled nursing facilities, and of course hospitals.
3. **The payers of care.** The organizations that fund healthcare outside of self-pay include the United States government, serving veterans, disabled, low income and senior Americans via the Veteran's Administration (VA), Medicaid and Medicare. There are also many private insurers offering Medicaid supplementary and Medicare replacements such as Medicare Advantage Plans. Other payers include commercial plans. These are your typical Health Maintenance or Preferred Provider Organizations (HMO/PPO) plans, which are generally available through employers, healthcare "co-ops" and of course the individual consumer market (ACA).

The healthcare ecosystem is possibly the largest of any and the most complex. It spans from all things technology,[4] research, pharmacy, and biopharma to care management, occupational medicine, long term living (nursing homes), hospice, and adjacent insurance products to sales and broker teams that promote the services/products. **This is great news for you as you grow in your career. Within the healthcare space, there seems to be no end to the options for great leaders**. We are all just glad you found your way here!

Essentially, as a healthcare leader, being aware of basic frameworks is essential, but are only truly useful to you if you understand how they end up playing out in the real world.

The Current Trends in the Game

A Backdrop First

In 2015, The Robert Woods Foundation introduced **"the Culture of Health" (CoH) action model** to inform its major grant-making decisions in the United States. The goal of the CoH is to provide everyone in America a fair and just opportunity for health and well-being. What a beautiful thought. In the same themes as "follow the money, it is important to recognize that investments—whether from venture capital (VC) or grant-making organizations—are key drivers of trends. A grant is the primary function of how our

4 There are multiple books on technology, so I won't go there much, other than to highlight the importance of a leader having a strong base line of knowledge as well as being very well aware that every day you will be or should be "in the data." The more you know, the more confident you will feel as you try to understand and take action. The finance world has demonstrated that their money is on the healthcare tech and "digital health" space, and I support that fully. "Skate to where the puck is going," right? (As said by Wayne Gretzky, former Canadian hockey phenom.)

society funds research and innovation in healthcare. The National Institutes of Health (NIH) alone in 2022 invested $45 billion dollars in the category.[5]

The principles of the **Culture of Health (CoH) action model** are:

1. **Making health a shared value**
2. **Fostering cross-sector collaboration**
3. **Creating more equitable communities (yes please!)**
4. **Transformation of healthcare systems**

Not surprisingly, not as much has progressed in the 4th principle as they had hoped. Our US healthcare system is not focused, funded or prioritized on prevention. Therefore, change and transformation require a massive shift in structural systems. *We need to break apart some glaciers!* Here's the great news: I have seen firsthand some great organizations start the hard work to do this, so know there is support as you go through your journey. It will take community to break it down and rebuild.

Along with the CoH,[6] you may also have heard of the **Quintuple Aim,** illustrated below. This framework was introduced into our lexicon by Don Berwick from **The Institute for Healthcare Improvement (IHI)** back in 2007 (it was initially the "Triple Aim"). In 2014, the 4th was added (by Drs. Bodenheimer and Sinsky) due to a national cry to acknowledge the impact of stress in the profession on those providing the care. ***(A reminder here that the PEOPLE***

5 ncbi.nlm.nih.gov

6 The CoH model is research driven, so bringing that into actual practice is a bit challenging and, in fact, often difficult to justify within the context of the current healthcare system status quo.

should come first—ALWAYS!). The 5th was added in 2021 by the IHI after the pandemic made it clear that we needed to also include an Equity aim to our North Star.[7]

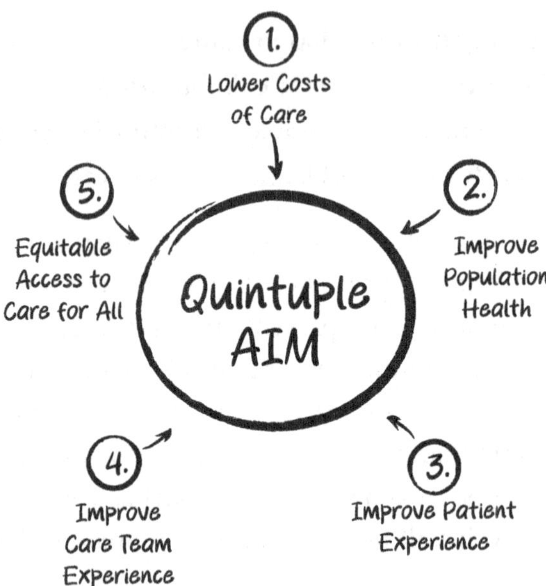

The intention was to have a national road map on what areas we needed to focus on in order to optimize our health system and therefore our overall population health. (As a healthcare leader, you or your organization may have designed your entire strategy around these goals.)

The Centers for Medicare and Medicaid (CMS) also use these areas as their focus in "Value-Based Care," which we will cover in depth later in the book. The bottom line here is a call to focus on outcomes (also known as Quality) which would

7 ncbi.nlm.nih.gov

then create the drive to lower costs (also known as Efficiency), and then to improve patient experiences and finally create an empowered care team.

It of course seems a bit ridiculous that we had to go through Covid-19 to get the systems to shift toward using existing technology to augment the healthcare system, but that's what happened. This accelerated us overnight to be able to use virtual tools and amazingly create a financial structure to ensure our care teams were paid and patients were taken care of. A terrific example of the quadruple aim in use if you ask me!

At that same time, our country finally took another, I would say, significant step ahead in talking openly about creating an equitable healthcare system. Somehow, it suddenly seemed obvious that our systems were not ensuring healthcare equity. Whether we're talking about the investments in greenspace, walkable streets, and safe neighborhoods or the access to healthy food and good and timely healthcare...pretty much all of it wasn't (and still isn't) up to a standard of excellence that we should expect in America. The great news is that this is now top of mind for nearly every organization I have worked with firsthand over the past few years, and I love it. **I hope you'll step into the ring to ensure that health equity continues to be addressed and maintains momentum within every key strategic discussion.**

As you think through the forces that bring about change, think of the magnitude of the pandemic and what that meant. Think about what it took to get our eyes and ears understanding what was going on with health equity right in front of us. For those of us who had been in the industry for some time, it was easy to see our failures immediately. We lost valuable time, and so many people were hurt. Lives were lost.

It's a national imperative that we ask ourselves:

- **How can we create massive shifts more quickly and without so much pain?**
- **How can we boldly lead and bring about a unified approach to taking on clear needs?**
- **What tools can we use?**
- **How can we ensure the best care for all people?**

I really appreciated this thought from David Blumenthal, MD, internationally admired healthcare leader and former president of the Commonwealth Fund:

"Health policies matter to people's day-to-day lives. For generations, federal, state and local leaders have made policy choices that have produced worse health outcomes for people of color, including economics, oppression, residential segregation, and failing to invest in the places where people of color live and work. Policy decisions have also affected access to and quality of health services available to racial and ethnic groups. There is no question that healthcare services are an important source of observed inequities."

AI in Healthcare

It is obvious now that the use of healthcare AI will be that next massive propeller. AI's integration into healthcare holds immense potential for more efficient, accurate, and equitable care delivery, but success will depend on addressing its challenges responsibly.

The following are some key AI innovations happening in healthcare today:

- With precision medicine, AI can analyze large datasets, such as genetic information and medical histories, to create personalized treatment plans.
- When it comes to administrative efficiency, AI automates routine tasks, such as billing, scheduling, and patient record management. This reduces the workload on healthcare staff.
- With imaging and pathology, AI-powered tools like computer vision improve the speed and accuracy of diagnostics in radiology and pathology to identify anomalies like cancer or fractures with high precision.
- Virtual assistants and chatbots provide 24/7 patient support, answer queries, and assist with medication reminders.
- For the purposes of predictive analytics, AI predicts patient surges and resource needs, helping hospitals allocate staff and equipment more effectively.
- AI makes remote monitoring possible. AI-integrated wearables track vital signs in real-time, allowing for early intervention in conditions like diabetes or heart disease.
- AI accelerates drug development by analyzing data to identify potential compounds, simulate clinical trials, and predict patient outcomes. This drastically cuts time and costs.
- AI-powered telemedicine platforms expand access to quality care in remote or underserved areas.
- Language translation and adaptive interfaces make healthcare more inclusive.

Much of what we will cover in the book will have some component of AI which is going to be fascinating to watch and be a part of. It is imperative that our healthcare leaders look at both the upsides and challenges (as well as potential blind spots) of our uses of these incredible advancements.

Trends and the Direction of the Healthcare Winds

Now that we know what some of the foundational driving forces are, we'll dive into some healthcare issues that should seem familiar to you. They are topics you want to tackle as a new healthcare leader. (It will be interesting to see how these topics change throughout the years…).

Here is my top 10 list:

Top 10 Areas of Change for Healthcare

1. Mental Health and Wellness

> **"Mental health costs the US economy more than $280 Billion annually, stymying investment, productivity, and wealth accumulation, among other measures of progress,"**
>
> **—Columbia Business School, May 2024**

Nearly every person I know is facing mental health challenges in some area of their lives, and in my recent experience, nearly 1 in 3 patients, if not more, are actively seeking support. Sometimes all that's needed is someone to talk to about life challenges, and sometimes—more often than I'd like—someone is going through something as serious as having suicidal thoughts. All ages are experiencing this, including elementary children. The latest data from the National

Institute of Health (NIH) from 2022 indicates 20 percent of those aged 3-17 are in this category. It may have always been a need but now it's being talked about, and that's a good thing. For the healthcare leader, it's a trend and one in need of solutions to scale successfully.

2. Team Member Shortages (Clinical Positions Especially)

The Association of American Medical Colleges shared a 2021 study highlighting that in the United States there would be a shortfall of 37,800 to 124,000 physicians by 2034.[8]

"The demand by 'Baby Boomers' will outpace its supply" is the central theme. Additionally, Definitive Healthcare conducted a 2023 study showing that there's more to it than physicians. We can include others, but of prime concern are the Medical Assistants (MAs). For those of you who don't know, the MAs are the "go-to" staff in most all medical clinics. They have a broad range of skills from rooming patients to giving immunizations to drawing laboratories and providing an exceptional experience. A good MA is pure gold if you ask me, and I have worked with some of the best. The Bureau of Labor Statistics predicts that the employment of MAs will grow nearly 20 percent before 2029. Needless to say, our core clinical care team is at risk, and it's an area we should all have top of mind. ***(Now, back to that advice I am going to inject frequently: People first, my friends...)***

8 (Ref: AAMC: Complexities of Physician Supply and Demand projections from 2019-2034)

3. Health Equity Strategies

The basic thinking here is to ensure you truly understand the need for health equity by understanding our various cultures and the socio-economic forces that drive their healthcare needs, wants and desires. Essentially, meeting people where they are, and ensuring that you, the team, and the organization you represent are acknowledging their realities and putting in systems and processes to ensure they have an opportunity for equitable healthcare.

I have a dear friend who is a lactation nurse. She has shared endless stories of the difference in expectation in the birthing and newborn care process of the multiple cultures she serves. Ten years ago, that wasn't something her hospital or her profession were focused on and it was not an expectation. Today, it's all about, "How can we provide the best care for all people?"

In many cases, care is only available until 5 pm. If you are a single parent or work in a profession without access to alternate hours, you may not have access to needed care for your family. Sometimes it is as obvious as this, yet as a profession we have often missed the mark. Let's do better together!

4. Technology

From virtual care to medical devices...

From the basic electronic medical record (EMR) to business intelligence tools...

From remote patient monitoring tools (RPM) to basic transcription services...

Nearly all of the tools we work with are advancing in technology every moment. They are the very foundation of transformation in the healthcare industry. As shared above, artificial intelligence (AI) is front and center, and we can expect it to be an engagement point for every part of our technology and operational systems. This area is absolutely thrilling to see.

5. Aging Consumers

The aging population of today is healthier than other generations according to many headlines. At the same time, consumers are willing to invest in wellness and areas that they perceive to contribute to healthy aging. The advent of advanced technologies and the recognition by healthcare leaders that patient experience is king has created some interesting progress here, specifically from the leadership of the Medicare Advantage organizations who are keenly focused on providing the best care for our nation's seniors, those 65 and older.

In this category, look for the continued growth of experience forward models to attract seniors to new primary care offerings and a return to home based care offerings which create personalized and more accessible care to meet the consumer where they are.

6. Wellness

There is a national movement in wellness. There are so many great resources and solid research to demonstrate that this is a trend that is going to continue to gain momentum. **Lifestyle Medicine and Food as Medicine will be strong drivers in**

this area of healthcare. (We will be diving into this later in the book!)

I want to offer an example in this area to drive the point home. I was so proud of the physician & leadership team at Prosano Health/Blue Cross and Blue Shield of Arizona. When we were standing up the care delivery organization, I assumed we would launch our foundational population health team around the well-known and industry accepted "Centers of Excellence" model for our patients with chronic disease conditions. This would look like creating a Diabetes Center of Excellence, a Cardiovascular Center of Excellence, etc. Our lead physician felt differently and led the team to take a step back and remind ourselves that we were given the opportunity to create a contemporary model of care, and did not necessarily need to be governed by the standards of the past. Essentially, the team was given a white board to create a model that they believed would give our patients the best outcomes and healthier lives overall. It was then so clear, that we should start with PREVENTION at the forefront of the model. Ultimately, we launched a Center of Excellence on Lifestyle Medicine and specifically homing in on Food as Medicine. **I hope that you will always remember to take a step back and ask yourself if the path you are on is the best for your patients (and team).** Such great leadership.

7. New and Improved Value-Based Care

Maybe we need another name, but this essentially means great outcomes, happy consumers and a viable payment system they can afford. As I shared above, this is one of the reasons I am writing this book. Value-Based Care is all over the place. For some reason, many in the industry continue to reference

"Patient Centered Medical Home," (PCMH) when describing their VBC initiatives. Friends, that is so old school—the iPhone came out the same year PCMH was introduced!

True Value-Based Care requires a complete overhaul of the systems and financial structures that support our system today. PCMH is a function of that and one step in the right direction. Today's VBC Model is committed to patient care and has created systems and processes to ensure this happens. They are rewarded by both providing exceptional care and receiving higher payments (intended to support the infrastructure needed) for their work. Everyone wins, especially the patient.

As I write this, sadly, a very low percentage of providers are at any significant level of true Value-Based Care population health management. The ones that are are known as the best in the business, and for good reason. This trend will continue to drive our industry. Knowing the full details of this is as important as knowing how you yourself are paid.

8. Pharmacy Overhauls

Along with tech, this is one we aren't going to dive into in this book due to the largeness of the topic; however, I would be remiss to not include it as a trend driving our world. It would be wise to understand the role of Pharmacy Benefit Managers (PBM) such as Optum and what is going on in the private sectors (i.e., Mark Cuban's Cost Plus Drug Company). There is much effort in the space trying to help us all understand and keep a measure of control over pharmacy drug costs and the impact on the average American family. This topic breaches into ethics and often brings about passionate opinions and national discourse. We need strong, committed and ethical leaders to be a part of the pharmaceutical industry like never before.

9. Health Policy

Health policy has always and will always drive trends and focus in the healthcare space. Everything from the CMS Innovation Center to the CDC response to the Covid-19 pandemic to the latest unexpected Measles outbreak falls into this category. In short, health policy in our country is a complex interplay of laws, regulations, and public health strategies (managed at the national and state levels), that share the goal of ensuring our citizens have access to quality healthcare. This is perhaps my least favorite due to the sheer size and complexity, but as a healthcare leader, it is a must have on the list of trends, as key components change often which creates a downstream impact on our daily work lives.

10. Strategic Partnerships with All Players to Solve Our Toughest Problems, Invest in Research, Etc.

One of the most exciting trends to watch are the strategic partnerships that unfold in the healthcare space. When health plans come together and there is investment in technology, for example, we all win. When providers join the health systems to create solutions for a local community, it can be beautiful. Think about the example of a payer and provider group partnering to open a surgery center in an area desperate to address access. (Not necessarily by acquisition, but by a business arrangement that supports a unified approach to improve patient care.) Those of you with super creative and innovative minds, we need your focus here more than ever!

I get excited about WHAT'S POSSIBLE! I hope you do as well!

The Big 3 (In Summary)

- The primary "playing field" is composed of the Patient, Provider and the Payer.
- Following the "money" in healthcare research across our country is useful for understanding what is driving today's work. Many nonprofit and government organizations have their hand in framing our focus.
- Trends in our population and technology mainly drive the conversations around strategy development. It is critical to always be a student of trends. If you are gifted with an innovative mind, we need you thinking about how to enter new territories here to meet healthcare's biggest challenges.

"Three things in human life are important. The first is to be kind. The second is to be kind. And the third is to be kind."

—Henry James

Chapter 3

Who Is Doing Something Cool?

"Let's do something SPECIAL."

—Patrick Mahomes (IMO the best quarterback in history!)

I have a phrase I use when talking about culture that I pulled from my hometown team's, the KC Chiefs, 2019 Superbowl run: **"Let's Do Something Special."** It is the phrase Patrick Mahomes used to inspire his team on the sidelines. It was a beautiful display of passion—and that, my friends, is what it takes: passion!

I like to ask, "Who is doing something cool?" as a spin-off of this phrase to bring to mind being in awe at the innovations of the healthcare industry.

Chapter three is all about who is doing something cool, so let's get started by talking about what's fun out there in this wild healthcare adventure.

There is much more to the profession than hospitals and physician's offices. Most of us grew up going to the doctor's at least once a year for our annual checkup. Most early career healthcare leaders, physicians and advanced practitioners imagine they will end up in a hospital or a traditional office setting supporting or providing traditional patient care.

When I speak to those exploring the idea of the profession, they have no idea of the vastness of the world they are considering. So, for this section, I will highlight some of the more innovative leaders and organizations that will open your mind to the next level.

One Medical, Iora, Amazon, Galileo

I want to start with someone who I think is one of the most innovative leaders in the space. Tom Lee is a physician that demonstrated his enterprising vision early on as a founder of the mobile-reference tool for providers, Epocrates, back in 1999. He then launched an innovative primary care model, One Medical, in 2007, selling that eventually to Amazon for $3.9 billion in July 2022. He is now leading another start-up, Galileo, which aims in part to serve as a population tool enabling 24/7 access to multi-specialty care on a mobile device.

It is a great idea to go research Dr. Lee a bit, and I'd start with listening in on some YouTube videos. He talks in a way that makes you challenge the status quo and consider what might happen if we flipped the current industry script upside down and rethought the model. It's nothing short of inspiring.

Before it was on everyone's mind, One Medical had the goal of creating a healthcare experience truly for the consumer, and I would say also designed for the provider. The model, similar to a concierge model, aimed to provide excellent care with enhanced communication with your provider team to enable better outcomes. The model demonstrated that it met a real need in our largest metropolitan cities, because there are a lot of people that don't want to receive care in the typical way, such as sitting in waiting rooms experiencing a long wait for an annual physical.

Dr. Lee early on wanted to try to figure out if somehow you could scale that model for larger populations, including seniors and those that don't have good access today for socio-economic or geographic reasons. He was and is constantly assessing the environment—the player and the technology—and contemplating ways to bring this vision to life.

He was able to forge strategic relationships and partnerships to help enable a new and better system of care. He invested in Iora Healthcare, a leader in the senior care space, in order to capture that intelligence and momentum. Dr. Lee was then driven to start to explore what more technology could do; thus, Galileo is his current focus. This type of innovation will allow us to reach into the areas and communities in rural America that, in many cases, desperately need healthcare solutions to meet the needs of their populations. I always follow him, as he is a wonderful example of the creativity and the commitment it takes to achieve progress; as incremental as it might be, it is what is changing the world.

Hinge Health

Two years ago, I found out about a private digital health company called Hinge Health. It was last valued after a Series E funding round in October of 2021 at $6.2 billion.[9] At the

9 businessinsider.com

time this book was in production, Hinge actually went public, creating the need to modify the content. It's an exciting time and reveals to us where the future is going.

Hinge is one of the most creative and interesting companies I have encountered, and based on their funders, I'm far from alone in my assessment. Their model is bringing forward the next evolution of care to our front doors. Hinge is taking on the high cost of the MSK (musculoskeletal) space (physical therapy and adjacent) for our nation's payers. MSK happens to be one of the largest drivers of cost for a payer. With the aging population and the increase in sports participation of all ages, this number will no doubt go up. Ensuring we scale these types of critical services requires innovation—and Hinge is on the frontline in their field. They have the ability to improve outcomes and reduce cost (driven by surgical intervention) by enabling technology and innovation to improve adherence and access.

I was able to try it for a shoulder issue and found it to be incredible. (I should insert here that I am typically skeptical about this type of technology, so I had little expectation and frankly couldn't imagine how they could personalize it.) I initially met with the physical therapist after they sent me a box, complete with what I needed. Just like a normal doctor's visit, she asked questions and then she showed me the tools and the exercises that I would be doing. The tech is ingenious; it allows them to see if I'm doing the movement correctly and adjust and educate as needed. We had ongoing coaching touch base sessions, and lo and behold, my pain went away without additional intervention.

Hinge is available through many employer health plan options right now and perhaps at some point will be a more "retail" offering. Keep an eye on Hinge, Sword and similar companies that intend to optimize our digital tools, create personalized experiences and reduce the cost of care for both the patient and the payer.

Transcarent

I first met Glen Tullman when he was the CEO of Allscripts. We were one of the pioneer groups adding an EMR to our practice, and Allscripts did a fantastic job of serving mid-sized practices, providing both an exceptional product and experience during a massive shift for our provider team and staff. Glen has gone on to be what some may refer to as a serial entrepreneur, and in all cases, he is clearly on a personal mission to bring forward a better world.

Glen's most recent role is that of founder of Transcarent, a digital health company focused on creating navigation tools for people to easily find high quality and affordable healthcare. Their solution is innovative in that the model is a direct model to large employer groups and is intended to tackle the employer-sponsored benefits space. As a healthcare leader, depending on your role, you may never have a clear path to the knowledge of the underpinnings of how your patients get their care paid for. The entire payer and employer space is a large part of our health system and one that a wise leader will ensure they understand. Transcarent is a terrific example of a starting place for learning.

Premera Blue Cross, Blue Cross and Blue Shield of KC, Blue Cross and Blue Shield of Arizona

I saved the best for last, based on my personal experience. I wasn't sure you could do something "cool" in the primary care space, but I was wrong. It sounds basic, but it's anything but. The new integrated payer provider models are quietly creating ripples that I believe will change the current landscape. I am speaking to examples such as Premera's Kinwell care centers in Washington State and Blue Cross and Blue Shield's (Kansas City and Arizona) Spira Care and Prosano care centers. Their early work is remarkable. The entire goal is to improve health outcomes and patient experience by capitalizing on the power of the payer and the power of the provider by bringing them together as true partners with a unified goal.

One of the greatest challenges for patients is often being able to find a primary care provider—and one that can see them or their family members within a reasonable amount of time and cost. These models were created to deliver on access, with many offering a $0 access fee for their patients for basic services (think the visit, laboratory testing, vaccinations, basic procedures, etc.) with the goal of ensuring barriers are minimized and that their primary care team can quarterback their care across the entire ecosystem. These models were curated after deep research, which included hearing from both consumers and providers. The design of these models was created to care for the most important factors and ensure the highest quality outcomes.

In these models, patients can focus on their whole health (including mental health and well-being) while experiencing timely access to providers, actual guidance and perhaps the best part, **advocacy**, as they navigate specialists and hospital care needs. This reduces frustration overall. Truly integrated models don't require you to share your insurance card every single time you visit or ask you to repeat your patient history multiple times.

These models are an even better experience for the care team as they aren't burdened with needing to know the details of every payer in the market. Additionally, they can actually provide the care they want to provide, giving more time and attention to the patient and helping them achieve their personal health goals.

The Gritty Stuff: Going Deeper

There is so much here, and I hope you will get excited with me as we power through some remarkable work that is altering our industry. It is a pivotal time in healthcare, and the advancements over your and my lifetime will most certainly create a better world. What's not to love about that notion? Envisioning that is enough to keep us motivated every day and to put in the good work necessary for progress. The following areas we will cover are intended to give you a broad view of the healthcare world, and who knows, many of you may end up being a part of or leading in one of these incredible areas.

Precision Medicine (Think Genomic Testing and Personalized Drugs)

As you can imagine, a one-size-fits-all approach is not the most effective way to deal with just about anything. If you have a sibling or have children yourself, you know that what works for one doesn't typically work for the other. We have to adjust. So, of course, we should have been on top of this category centuries ago, versus just 2 decades ago. At any rate, here we stand and it's worth diving into… but first, some background that helps us grasp the current state.

When Francis Collins, former director of the National Human Genome Research Institute, testified before Congress in 2003 on the controversial topic of sequencing the human genome, he introduced **personalized medicine** as a new concept. He predicted that in 10 years, personalized medicine would allow physicians to employ predictive genetic tests so that each of us could learn of our individual risks for future illness and practice more effective health maintenance and disease prevention. The once popular 23andMe was founded just 3 years later in 2006. The company's mission was to help people access and benefit from their genetic information. I am sure many of you have taken advantage of this advancement and I personally have found great value in optimizing my own health. Game-changing.

Since 2003, researchers and industry leaders in health and medicine have driven at least 100,000 molecular tests and 350 molecularly targeted medicines to the market. More than half of all clinical trials in cancer care are now for drugs that are targeted to patients with certain genetic characteristics. In 2020, the advancements brought Collins to introduce the idea that gene-based designer drugs are likely to be available soon for conditions like diabetes, Alzheimer's disease, hypertension, and many other disorders. There is truly so much to dive into here and it will change disease management as we know it today. With the promises of AI, I expect this area to accelerate greatly. I can't wait to see what happens here!

This seems like a good place to capture the major categories of personalized medicine:

The Top 3 Categories of Personalized Medicine

1. **Precision Oncology:** Researchers are actively identifying the molecular fingerprints of various cancers and using them to divide cancer's once-broad categories into deeper levels of specificity.
2. **Cancer Immunotherapy:** Decades of NIH research has led to several types of cancer immunotherapy drugs.
3. **Pharmacogenomics:** A significant goal of precision medicine is to implement this strategy broadly—focusing on the right drug at the right dose at the right time for the right patient.

So, Who Are the Key Players?

As you can imagine, big pharma almost has to be behind any new developments in medicine, along with research-based organizations, such as the NIH. A recent article by Jonathan Smith, a freelance science journalist, shares that the top 5 players are Alnylam Pharmaceuticals, Biogen, BioMarin, Johnson & Johnson and Novartis.[10]

There are others; a great deep dive can be found by following Precision Medical Group. Blackstone, the country's leading asset manager, purchased Precision Medical Group back in 2012 and clearly believes that this will be a story for all of our futures. For those interested in healthcare financing or investing, follow the money here. This tells you volumes about where we are headed as future healthcare leaders.[11]

10 https://www.insideprecisionmedicine.com/news-and-features/five-key-precision-medicine-players-with-products-in-the-market/

11 https://www.precisionmedicinegrp.com/news/-

Regenerative Medicine

Another amazing category is that of regenerative medicine. The idea can be a bit of challenge to think through. I found this helpful:

> **"Regenerative medicine may become the most powerful tool available to improve the human condition. *Science has shown it can achieve the goal of using the body's own substances and cells to repair, restore, and rejuvenate it."* (2003)[12]**

One of the more common aspects of regenerative medicine that you have likely heard is the use of stem cell therapy. Stem cell therapy uses our own stem cells to repair our own cartilage wear and tear and address disease in some cases. There is some indication that there is an approximate 90% success rate in this area. [13]

Another exciting use case is that great success in this category has been experienced for autism with an incredible 85-90% seeing improvement.[14] For certain blood cancers, a success rate of 60-70% has been achieved.[15]

This progress is remarkable, but it will require ongoing research. For this reason, regenerative medicine, in many forms, is here to stay.

---

12 https://www.brookings.edu/articles/regenerative-medicine-a-future-healing-art/Regenerative

13 https://www.arthritis.org/health-wellness/treatment/joint-surgery/preplanning/the-future-of-joint-repair

14 https://www.abtaba.com/blog/stem-cell-therapy-for-autism-success-rate

15 https://www.dvcstem.com/post/stem-cell-success-rate.

Robotic Surgery

Robotic surgery has been around since at least 1985, when the first surgical robot, the PUMA 560, was used in a brain biopsy procedure. The original goal was simply to reduce hand tremors from the physician which could impact surgical performance. Fast forward to our current reality, where robotic surgery is now done approximately 17 percent of the time according to StrategicMarketResearch.com. This includes cardiothoracic, colorectal, gynecology and head and neck surgery—and the list is growing. Here's what the Surgical Robotics Market Research Report had to say about the prevalence of robotic surgery:

"The surgical robotics market has experienced a remarkable surge, reaching a value of $78.8 billion in 2022. Projections indicate a continued growth trajectory with a steady annual increase of 9.1%, set to hit $188.8 billion by 2032."

My guess is that this is a low estimate. In January 2025, the Consumer Technology Association hosted the annual Consumer Electronics Show, (CES), known as the most powerful tech event in the world. Here they introduced a mind-blowing array of new robots driven by AI. This event illustrated the exponential growth we will see here… Stay tuned! [16]

Some additional areas for you to pay attention to within this category:

- Enhanced precision with 3D visualization tools
- Miniaturized surgical robots for the tiniest areas
- Remote surgery breakthroughs

16 https://www.thesurgicalclinics.com

Imagine being able to serve rural markets remotely with a critical surgery!

Bioprinting and the 3D Printing of Custom Prosthetics and Organs

And finally—something that truly is hard for my logical brain to comprehend—the innovation of being able to print body parts and even an organ. Wow.

Bioprinting in medicine uses proteins, cells, and nutrients to make human tissues to treat injury and disease. It can produce organs for transplants using bioinks combined with living cells for 3D printing. This process mimics our functional tissue for use in regenerative medicine and drug testing, making it possible to replace or repair tissues and organs that are damaged.[17]

This includes 3D printing of new corneas, skin and bone grafts, and even full organs such as the heart, kidneys and liver. It's mind-blowing, really. Once this is mastered, there is no end to how we can repair and replace body parts with effective artificial ones.

According to Conor & Stewart in March of 2024, 3D printing facilities were increasingly becoming a part of the hospital landscape in the US In 2019 with 113 hospitals in North America having a centralized 3D printing facility. **Can you imagine the progress this represents?** This gives hope to so many, as there are over 100,000 Americans on average waiting for an organ transplant.[18]

---

17 https://www.upmbiomedicals.com/solutions/life-science/what-is-3d-bioprinting

18 https://www.psu.edu

> **Fun Fact:** Ever get hit in the mouth with a ball or know someone who has? Yikes. Good news….Dental implants were one of the first medically approved uses of 3D technology. A 2021 study in the Journal of the American Academy of Orthopedic Surgeons concluded that 3D printing has "significantly impacted bone and cartilage restoration and has the potential to completely transform how we treat patients with debilitating musculoskeletal injuries."

Another exciting advance is the use of 3D printing to improve how custom prosthetics fit and function. The technology has become accessible and affordable, and some are using it to create their own limbs. Incredible! The organization e-NABLE is a global community of volunteers who have created more than 10,000 prosthetic hands and arms for people worldwide.[19]

Now, let's talk about other medical tech innovations to get excited about!

Immersive Simulation Technologies

Immersive simulation technologies are transforming the landscape of healthcare training. We will discuss later the importance of training and onboarding for all roles and this represents life changing innovation. These cutting-edge solutions including using virtual reality (VR) simulations of surgical procedures and augmented reality (AR) applications for anatomy exploration, mimic real life medical situations and provide students a safe environment to practice and perfect their skills.

---

19 https://www.enablingthefuture.org

Gamification for Engaging Learning

The concept of gamification became a common term in strategy sessions in my world about 10 years ago. Keeping in line with this section, gamification has also made considerable strides in recent years in many areas including learning. Gamification incorporates game-like elements, such as point systems, leaderboards, and rewards, into training modules. Healthcare professionals are motivated to participate and achieve mastery actively and in a fun team or solo environment, allowing teachers to customize learning to a student's preferential style.

Challenges as We Move Forward

As you can see, there are significant opportunities for new models and tremendous clinical innovations and progress being made. **Imagine the excitement in the boardrooms, care centers and labs as they reach new levels of improved outcomes and understanding.**

That said, we should recognize the challenges that are always a part of the system and be educated on how to navigate the waters in these complex areas of healthcare.

The chief among these are **reimbursement and safety issues.** As we rapidly evolve technology into a highly regulated field, some of the issues that require resolution include:

1. What will reimbursement models be? We have to look upstream at how we pay for these innovations and decide who should pay. (Patients, payers, etc.)
2. How will the governing regulatory bodies pivot to both meet demand and the assessment of potential

> risks wisely? How will they know how to do this? Who really has the knowledge to make strong decisions in such a new world of progress?

I'm sure there are others. This is merely a glimpse into the daunting task that is bringing true progress to life. We are right to be excited and optimistic, and wise to understand why progress doesn't typically meet our expectations in terms of speed to market in most cases.

The next chapter will help you understand one way we can sometimes do this faster: strategic partnerships.

The Big 3 (In Summary)

- **Follow amazing innovators such as Hinge, and Transcarent…Don't stop doing this throughout your career.**
- **Having a strong awareness of clinical innovation and the research advancing medicine is a core responsibility for healthcare leaders.**
- **When bringing forward innovation yourself, be sure to establish clear frameworks that ensure understanding of the reimbursement and safety issues that impact your organization or work.**

"If you want to go fast, go alone. If you want to go far, go together."

—African Proverb

Chapter 4

Strategic Partnerships

"Apple Watch Nike+ takes performance tracking to whole new level and we can't wait to bring it to the world's largest community of runners."

-Apple

First Up—What Is a Strategic Partnership?

A strategic partnership is when two organizations (an organization could literally be an individual as well, such as a solopreneur) come together for the greater good. As in the quote above… take something to a whole new level. That is a good way to think about the opportunity. There are quite a few popular consumer examples of this, like:

- McDonalds and Coca-Cola
- Nike and Apple
- GoPro and Red Bull
- Taco Bell and Doritos
- Target and Magnolia

What is interesting is that although there is an understanding that strategic partnerships are designed to help both parties achieve greater success, most healthcare leaders don't often consider them as essential when crafting their own business plans. This needs to change! My career has demonstrated repeatedly just how important actively pursuing strategic partnerships is to accomplish the important goals of both optimizing our team and the care we desire to provide. Truly embracing appropriate strategic partnerships is not only an important part of a healthcare leader's playbook, but it's also one of the more fun and exciting tactics to achieving strategic goals. In short, we simply don't have time to do it all, so bringing in like-minded partners to solve our toughest challenges helps us get to making a meaningful difference faster and likely much better. Here's a brief framework of finding the right partner:

Even when I was the CEO of a privately owned mid-sized medical practice, (250 staff, 9 locations, roughly 200,000 annual patient visits), the leadership team had a bi-annual "Innovation" strategy session, in which we considered all manner of creative ideas with the goal to meet the needs of our patients and achieve our bottom-line financial goals. Our results included laboratory, payer, vendor and even community partnerships.

Partnerships are absolutely necessary when your organization isn't able to achieve its goals due to a lack of resources, or it isn't the best decision to go it alone when solving for a need. Bringing into the conversation who is out there doing what we need better than we could and being open to partnering with like-minded people are the first steps. As a healthcare leader, it's important to always ask oneself, "Who can we partner with that would help us reach more people faster?"

> **Pro Tip:** Gather insights on strategic partnerships across industries. Then, use YouTube commercials or brand campaigns with which to pitch your ideas to the team during meetings. (I love to use my hometown Kansas City Chiefs as an inspiration!)

I had the good fortune while working with Humana of being on a team that aimed to create, in some cases, and also lead ongoing strategic partnerships. Bruce Broussard, Humana's new CEO at the time, aimed early on in his new role to bring the company forward in the care delivery space. He recognized that being successful over the next few decades in American healthcare meant extending Humana from being a financier of care to an organization committed to creating healthier communities.

He immediately started developing a multi-solution approach to make this a reality—and one of those was developing strategic partnerships. Some of these solutions included partnerships with private primary care groups such as MCCI or EliteHealth in South Florida. There were also venture capital (VC) backed startups such as Iora Primary Care and Oak Street Health. Humana was actually the first to bring senior primary care into the retail realm with a Walgreens partnership. Humana's efforts demonstrate the power of partnerships and our ability as leaders to reach our goal of providing the best care for the communities we serve.

The 3 Types of Strategic Partnerships

The following three distinct types of partnerships were outlined by Forbes:

Product Partnership

Product partnerships help accelerate the product roadmap, build collaborative products (and services) and defend against competition.

Two organizations who bring their products together is what makes for a Product Partnership. For example, Starbucks has had strategic partnerships with Evolution, Teavana and others. This brings in products that are not their own but can help serve the growth needs of their organization. Health plans and provider groups have come together, like Anthem and CareMore Health, to provide care for members. **Why go it alone when there are others doing it already—and *better* than you likely could if you were on your own?**

Channel Partnership

Channel partnerships extend the organization's ability to reach a broader market including breaking into new specific geographic or vertical markets.

Have you ever received an email that said something like because you had an American Express Card you were able to access concert tickets on Ticketmaster earlier than others? **This is an example of a Channel Partnership.** This enables Ticketmaster to access clients of American Express. A basic healthcare example would be that in many cases your medical supply representative/salesperson will introduce you to new products. The manufacturer, for example, of a new exam table format likely doesn't have the money to fund their own salesforce, so they use the top medical supply organizations as their proxy and thus create a channel for their product distribution.

Brand Partnership

Brand partnerships help organizations amplify their presence to drive awareness across new and existing customer segments.

For over 15 years, the American Heart Association and the National Football League (NFL) have come together with a goal of improving the health of our nation's youth, via their NFL PLAY 60 program. **This is an example of a Brand Partnership.**

Keep in mind the ways in which one partnership can tackle multiple business needs. A strong partnership just might be the smartest business decision you make both for your main role and also for any boards you happen to serve on. As a rising healthcare leader, your strategic planning retreat should have an open space for whiteboard thinking in this key category.

As we move toward our "Mini Masterclass" section, I hope your brain is starting to fire on all things "possibility." Each of the topics we will cover need fresh thinking and a willingness to understand the foundations in order to ensure strength in leadership and a strong jumping off point.

The Big 3 (In Summary)

- Strategic Partnerships are a critical part of your strategy as a healthcare leader—no matter what size or type of organization you serve.
- There are three types of partnerships to consider, including Product, Channel and Brand. Exploring each is a good idea.
- Using other industry examples upon which to establish your brainstorming session (I like to refer to them as "innovation sessions") is a great way to get the team thinking creatively.

"Love cannot remain by itself—it has no meaning. Love has to be put into action and that action is service."

—Mother Teresa

Part II

Mini Masterclasses

The intent of this section is to provide a short study of what I consider to be the "must know" categories for a healthcare leader.

Masterclass has become a common word, thanks to the new learning website, Masterclass.com. But the first master class (it was two words until the new site came to life) took place in the realm of music and education. Today, they are as broad as there are topics to cover and people interested in going deep in their interests. Master classes can be for beginners or advanced students, which makes them a universal resource.

A few criteria are required for a master class, including:

- It is taught by an expert
- It is short and focused
- It carries more niche value[20]

Each of the six "mini masterclasses," as I am calling them, will have a learning objective of advancing your knowledge in that area with a real-life version of what is happening right now in 2025. The goal is to bring you into the boardroom. This way, you can clearly visualize where we are and how you as a healthcare leader can help us elevate our profession and advance good across the country.

---

20 https://www.LearnWorlds.com

Chapter 5

Our Team Masterclass #1: Culture at the Center of It All

"Every day, I strive to build the kind of company that my father never had a chance to work for, one that not only cares for its people, but gives them opportunities to be their best selves."

—Howard Schultz, founder of Starbucks

Badassery—A Technical Term

I had a call this morning with a former colleague I have a great deal of respect for. She is one of the most badass *and* kind leaders I have met over my career. Her approach since my first day engaging with her demonstrated her priority of being authentic, welcoming, kind and encouraging.

We were on a corporate call with over 200 people and the CEO was introducing me to the leadership team. I won't forget her genuine kindness. Out of the group of leaders on the call, she stood out, sending me a Teams message with a warm welcome, offering her support if I ever found myself needing anything. It wasn't much longer before I realized the strength of her overall leadership. She was an exceptional well-rounded leader and a true expert in her areas of the business. I fondly refer to this combination of brilliance and kindness as "badassery." A noble unofficial title goal for all to strive for!

This is of course a bit humorous, but the bottom line is that especially for women (and increasingly for men), if you lead with too much boldness (providing a strong point of view, giving clear direction, having honest conversations, especially too soon in a new role), you can be disregarded as difficult, and if you are too kind, you can be dismissed as not being a strong leader—thus not able to handle the tougher sides of the business. This is unfortunately the case, even when there are objective key metrics achievement. This colleague was both kind and exceptional in her work. That's what it takes to build a healthy culture that achieves the goals of the business.

It's been my goal as a leader to always lead with kindness, collaboration and relationship building. I have found that if you lead in this way, you will build trust and relationships with your team and be able to scale mountains that many teams cannot. I have always had one of the top employee or associate engagement scores in any organization I've been a part of, along with the result of dedicated teams achieving goals and objectives together. That alone is proof that this approach is one that breeds success. I hope you will boldly choose the path of "badassery" as a leader in the healthcare space. This is my most passionate topic, and I cannot wait to dive in. *In this game, there is nothing more important than leading with culture.*

What We Can Learn from the Best of the Best in Sports

There is no shortage of information on the importance of teams, so I'll assume you know that creating strong teams is a foundational minimum. We can look no further than the recent 2024 Olympic games, where gymnasts, basketball players, swimmers and track and field athletes demonstrated on the international stage the power of their teams in helping them achieve their personal goals as well as the collective team goals. Another example is of course professional sports, and as you already might have guessed, my favorite is American football and the National Football League. It's also important to include professional women's sports, whose popularity is (finally) on the rise in America.

Here are some renowned "people and culture" coaches and the key traits we should focus on to improve our own cultural skills. In this conversation, the term "people coach" will refer to those who prioritize the development and well-being of their players, as well as their own relationships to those players and their success on the field or court. These coaches are not only tactically sound but also excel in creating a supportive and inspiring environment.

Tony Dungy, Head Coach of the Indianapolis Colts when they won Super Bowl XLI

Renowned for his calm demeanor, integrity, and emphasis on character, Tony is known for **mentoring players not just on the field but in life, focusing on their personal growth and well-being.** Dungy's leadership style is rooted in his faith and a commitment to treating everyone with respect.

Pete Carroll, Head Coach of the Seattle Seahawks when they won Super Bowl XLVIII

He is famous for his **enthusiastic and positive approach.** He focuses on **creating a supportive and competitive environment where players are encouraged to be themselves.** Carroll emphasizes the importance of relationships, personal development, and maintaining a positive culture within the team.

Bill Walsh, Head Coach for the San Francisco 49ers and their three Super Bowl wins

His focus on leadership and developing his players and staff is significant. Walsh was known for **nurturing talent and empowering his coaches and players to grow and succeed, both on and off the field.** Walsh's coaching tree is one of the most extensive in NFL history. (Side note: his book, *The Score Takes Care of Itself*, is a must-read!)

Andy Reid, current Head Coach of the Kansas City Chiefs—who have won three Super Bowls under his leadership—and who also led the Philadelphia Eagles to a Super Bowl win

Andy is widely regarded for his excellence with his players. His leadership style is characterized by a combination of **respect, empathy, and a deep understanding of the game**. Because it's my favorite team, and it is such powerful information, I am going to share more deeply about his PEOPLE oriented approach:

Player Development/Mentorship

Reid is known for his ability to develop players. He has a strong track record of nurturing talent and helping players reach their full potential. Reid **empowers his players by giving them the confidence and tools** they need to succeed. He **tailors his coaching to the individual strengths** and needs of his players, allowing them to play to their strengths.

Strong Relationships

Reid builds **strong, trusting relationships** with his players. He treats them with respect and **values their input**, which **fosters a positive and collaborative team environment.** Reid is known for **his loyalty to his players, often giving them second chances and standing by them during tough times.** This loyalty has earned him great respect from his players and coaches.

Positive Culture

Reid **creates a supportive and inclusive team culture.** He is **approachable and maintains a positive demeanor**, which helps to keep morale high.

John Wooden, legendary UCLA basketball coach

John Wooden is perhaps the quintessential "people coach." Known for his "Pyramid of Success," Wooden **emphasized character, teamwork, and personal development. He believed in building individuals before building teams.**

Pat Summitt, legendary University of Tennessee Lady Volunteers basketball team

She is the winningest coach in NCAA Division I basketball history, with 1,098 career wins. Pat was a true legend. Her **people-centric approach** was renowned for its focus on **player**

development, both on and off the court. She emphasized discipline, hard work, and personal growth. Summitt **built strong, lasting relationships** with her players, **mentoring them through challenges and helping them succeed in their personal and professional lives.**

Becky Hammon, Head Coach of the Las Vegas Aces, Women's NBA

Hammon is known for her strong leadership and **ability to build relationships with her players. She focuses on creating a positive team culture**, developing her players' skills, and **empowering them both on and off the court.**

Not let's look at the traits these coaches have in common. **We can call them the Power 7:**

The "Power 7" Traits of Exceptional Leaders

1. They care... they are KIND!
2. They build relationships.
3. They empower.
4. They instill confidence (BELIEVE IN THEIR TEAM).
5. They focus on both the INDIVIDUAL and the TEAM.
6. They personally bring a positive attitude and elevate the team's energy.
7. They give their team the tools they need to contribute at their highest level.

Let's break these down into an application for the healthcare leader. It should be stated that this level of excellence is only achieved through the foundation of INTENTIONALITY. **A strong leader will find that prioritizing their people is their most important task any day, month, quarter or year. If they choose to focus first on projects, data, etc., and not the people, their ability to truly achieve greatness will be limited.**

The Power Seven

Power Theme #1: They care.

How you show caring is unique to you, and caring likewise in the other direction is received in a highly personal way by the range of people you lead. It's important to understand what your team values as behavior that shows you care. In fact, what one person thinks demonstrates caring, another may find annoying. I'll give you an example.

As a young leader, and before I launched into my healthcare career, I worked in telecommunications sales and then sales leadership. I was young and clearly needed some mentoring. I had a guy on my team that was the best salesperson in the region. He was awesome. The only opportunity I could see was that if he could get more organized, he would sell even more. Well, thankfully at that time, I'd say I was strong in that area. So, I came in on a weekend and organized his entire office. It looked amazing and I couldn't wait for Monday morning to get his reaction.

Let's just say it was everything I did NOT expect. He nicely asked if we could chat and proceeded to ask me how I would feel if someone came into my office and tossed papers and otherwise created a chaotic space. My head dropped and I knew immediately that my approach was wrong and going forward would not be welcomed by every person. He taught me a big lesson that day and I have never forgotten it. We are each distinct individuals from one another, and caring starts with understanding that first.

Over the years, I have gathered three areas of leadership to focus on in order to be able to put yourself in your team's shoes and truly show you care.

3 Focus Areas for Showing You Care as a Leader

1. **Personal growth:** This is a broad category. This includes learning the power of body language, understanding different cultural preferences such as how respect is demonstrated, and studying skills such as empathy and patience. If you are already strong in this category, keep fine tuning by asking those in your circle to call you out if you don't meet the mark. No matter what, never stop learning about yourself and how you can be a better leader.
2. **"Others" focused tools:** I am a big fan of leveraging analytics to help understand my team personality dynamics. My favorite has been the Culture Index tool and advisory firm which was recommended to me over a decade ago by Gina Danner, an amazing Kansas City business leader. Others, like Myers-Briggs and StrengthsFinder, provide similar information. (Culture Index provides a coach with their product, so as a leader that alone amplifies your game.) Using these types of tools to help truly understand personality types gives you powerful information as you learn how to optimize the team.
3. **YOUR TEAM:** Perhaps the best area to learn and grow here is with your team themselves. Asking them what demonstrates caring to them personally and giving you an example should be your first step in any leadership assignment. (I would suggest this not just with your team, but with your leaders, your peers or anyone that you will be working closely with.)

Power Theme #2: They build relationships.

When I first became a manager, I remember a conversation with my leadership team that cautioned me that I couldn't or shouldn't be going out to happy hour with the team now that I was their leader. I of course understood that, but I also realized that continuing to build on relationships was going to be central to any success I might have in this new role. As you can see, this one is nuanced. On one hand, you must find the balance of building a professional relationship while being authentic. Authentically caring to me is the hallmark of a relationship. True caring cannot be manufactured, and it has to be based on a mutual exchange. As a healthcare leader committed to excellence, caring about both the individual team members and the goals you are trying to achieve together is paramount.

When it comes to building professional relationships, my best advice is to start with growing your CARING muscles as we discussed above, and then begin to "earn your reps" by establishing routines that support your growth here. Here are two favorites:

Healthy 1:1s

I cannot speak enough about the profound power of ensuring you have an ongoing healthy dialogue with your team members in what I refer to as a "healthy" one on one (1:1). These mission critical sessions are THE place to build that core relationship and keep it ongoing in a systematic way. For example, I recommend these be calendared for the entire year as a part of your weekly routine.

I used to do mine, for example, every Tuesday and Thursday mornings. In fact, the entire leadership team did, so in that way, we all knew we were focused on our people at that time and not scheduling meetings over the most important part of our jobs. Healthy 1:1s provide the space to learn about how your team member is feeling and how you can support them best. It's the place to truly get to know them better.

You can even do one per month or week focused on the work they are engaged with, goal setting, barrier removal, etc., and another per month or week focused on personal development. Where do they want to go? How are they feeling? What's the one thing you can do to champion them? Take notes and always follow up, and in the next session, refer back to that dialogue to show you are listening and you genuinely want to be a good leader.[21]

Unfortunately, I need to spend a bit of time here. There are a couple of truths that I have found, and the second is the reason for the purposedly titled "Healthy 1:1. For me, this comes naturally and is also incredibly logical, so anything opposed to that dumbfounds me really, yet the way it plays out supports the fact that it's not quite that easy. Here's why.

MANY I have led—and I need to underscore MANY (as in MOST)—may agree and nod their heads that they understand and agree of the importance of these check-ins, but ultimately, they let their work rule their lives, versus establishing known systems designed to set them up for success (i.e., the *regular* 1:1 schedule). I have literally had to practically legislate that

21 As we've discussed, at least two a month will do, but it depends on team members' time in their role, where they are in their career goals, and what needs to be discussed.

these be completed—and that is no fun, I can assure you. If you want to be a transformational leader, you simply must be highly organized from the start—or starting today!—and in doing so, you build relationships which will help you to achieve massive success.

Another truth (and the most unfortunate one) is that many 1:1s are not done well. Without proper training to help establish strength here, far too often people progress in their careers without finding the true power here. A story here may be helpful.

I had a manager that worked for me a few years ago that was what I refer to as "legalistic" in nature. For example, if the employee manual said no blue hair, she'd promptly put a new employee on a corrective performance plan, without even considering that the associate was new, OR that many others had blue hair in other locations. I know that is silly, but as a leader, we can't always take what may be an ancient policy and enforce it without asking questions. She was very good, as you can imagine, at getting her 1:1s completed based on this checklist mentality; however, her team felt awful about them and shared that "it was like going into the principal's office every single time." Goodness—she even had them sign a form each time that verified that she completed the process! My friends, she missed the point and wasn't a leader on our team for much longer. The takeaway message here is to practice and role play this until you feel confident.

Management By Walking Around (AKA MBWA)

This term was made famous by Tom Peters, but it was coined back in the 1970s by Hewlett Packard's David Packard. As a young leader out of school, I started doing this on Fridays as it is typically a more casual day in many business environments. It means spending as much of the day as possible walking around and just checking in. "How was your week? Any highlights? Lowlights? Any weekend plans?"

This is the easiest and most fun part of my week. And as the motivational phrase goes: "Days turn into weeks, weeks into years and years into your lifetime." Essentially, do it well, as it all adds up.

Demonstrate that you care and let your team know before the weekend break that you and the organization are appreciative of the value they add and them as a person. Of course, this can be done at any time. As I have advanced in my career, sometimes I've only been able to be in a clinic or care center a couple of times a month… This would be my goal of the entire visit if at all possible.

In a Forbes article, author Joe McKendrick shared: "It's not just about being friendly. It's a way of keeping one's ear to the ground to understand what is really going on in the business." Such a great truth. Actively listening (and then following up if needed) is the single best use of time in my opinion.[22]

Power Theme #3: They empower.

Empowerment is a widely used term that honestly has been inappropriately used in my opinion. I say that because many like to say it's a core value of their organization, but often it is only given (and often it cannot be widely dispersed without proven actions) to a handful, leaving many on the team to roll their eyes.

22 (Forbes.com, 4/6/2020)

Empowerment of course is giving someone the agency, the permission, the power in a specific area. It's allowing the team to use their "voice" in a specific area. It takes a measure of trust to empower the team. Some ways I have actively used this includes everything from engaging a team to lead core areas that we are focused on, to challenging a rising leader to step into a leadership position in a specific campaign.

One of my favorites from the last few years was a team that was focused on helping our startup develop health equity strategies for our patients and community. I was at the formation meeting, but after that I wasn't at the table. They blew me away. They set up a farmer's market in our lobbies, created activities, and expanded the concept to our larger community events. They had so much fun, developed leadership skills and of course got the attention of the leaders, who of course went to some of those team members for enhanced leadership roles. One of my favorite empowerment strategies has been to assign (I always ask them first if this is a passion and of interest to them personally) someone hoping to become a leader or advance in their current leadership role to lead a campaign such as the American Heart Association's Go Red for Women Campaign, which is held every February, and/or their annual community Heart Walk. It's typically a fun assignment, and it helps me and them as we explore their strengths and how to continue to develop a strong base of core leadership skills.

Power Theme #4: They instill confidence.

Believe in your team! Can you imagine an NFL coach who did not believe in their team? How about a parent or caretaker that didn't believe in their child? I suppose it happens every day, sadly, but we need to believe in our team—hard stop. It's true that we get to handpick some of our team members, but often they are given to us as we step into a new role.

I'm the first to tell you that interviewing is hard. Even when we believe we have picked our next all-star, we can still fail to pick up on traits that are going to prove to be a challenge soon after they join the team. Nonetheless, we as leaders must develop a core skill of instilling confidence, even in the complex realities found in people management. Where to start?

I have always loved that little poem, "All I Really Need to Know I Learned in Kindergarten" by Robert Fulghum. It got me thinking how in order to truly honor people and instill confidence in them, we can appeal to the universal need to feel love that starts in childhood. We can look to the following principles from TheHighlyEffectiveTeacher.com for boosting a child's confidence and apply them to those we lead. This philosophy is the most effective I've found for truly bringing out the best in the team.

5 Ways to Boost a Child's Confidence

1. **Praise them for their efforts, not just their achievements.**
2. **Encourage them to take risks.**
3. **Help them build positive relationships.**
4. **Encourage them to take on new challenges.**
5. **Help them set and achieve goals.**[23]

Isn't that perfect? The most important part here for you to remember is that you must instill confidence in *everyone* you lead. Even your top performers (perhaps them more than

23 https://www.thehighlyeffectiveteacher.com

anyone) need someone to champion them; they need to know that you believe in them as they rise higher.

Power Theme #5: They focus on both the individual and the team.

This reinforces the importance of the Healthy 1:1s and then brings us to the important other key meeting, which is the TEAM MEETING. At some very regular interval (daily stand ups, weekly, monthly, quarterly planning, etc.), leaders must establish discipline around an established meeting schedule. It's typically a combination of those listed. There are so many ways to do this well—and a few key ways to really screw this up. Let's focus on the latter for this one.

How to Screw up an Established Meeting Schedule

1. The number one fail here is in not being consistent and one of the most common complaints I have seen on employee satisfaction surveys This would look like skipping or rescheduling meetings on a regular basis. The team needs that touchpoint where all team members hear a collective and unifying message. When we don't prioritize this, we are not able to achieve our goals, no matter how hard we try. This is Communication 101.
2. The second fail here is in not having or following a planned agenda. I recommend posting a standard agenda (with most topics recurring in each meeting) on Teams, or whatever system you use, and allowing team members to add topics.[24]

---

24 Please check this before the meeting to ensure you can cover these topics realistically, and if not, follow up with the individual who asked for it and develop a plan to address it. Some topics may be too sensitive to be in a group session, or not appropriate due to the existing schedule that day.

3. The third fail is not keeping these as concise as can be. The team needs to believe we value their time, and we can do this by having a plan and following it at least 85% of the time. We do need to allow flexibility, so I use the 85/15 rule, but do whatever works best for your team.

To add to this, the best way I've found to both emphasize the individual and the team is to inject fun into your meetings. Involve both guests and team members to lead certain aspects. In regard to "fun," a simple ice breaker round table (Think, "What is your favorite childhood candy?") goes a long way in learning about one another and creating a collaborative environment. Not all need an icebreaker, but if time permits, it's truly appreciated by the team.

Quarterly or annual meetings are a great opportunity to do more of this. Even hosting off-site events such as pickleball, bowling, etc., are terrific. On inviting others and engaging the team, organized team meetings are awesome to invite another department for a teaching moment and learning about other aspects of the organization. This adds a dynamic to the team meeting which people really appreciate. When one of your team members has been working on a project and it's time to share it, using time in the team meeting is a safe and ideal space to share!

Power Theme #6: They personally bring a positive attitude and elevate the team's energy.

As a healthcare leader, you have been given a unique gift to create a thriving environment. Think back to your favorite teachers, coaches, principals... what is something they have in common? For most, they can recall a high level of passion and energy coming from these people. It's not always a "rah rah" cheerleader type energy, but it is energy that brings forward positive results.

I have my own ongoing science experiment (if you will) in my family, having fraternal triplet sons. They couldn't be more different, and the introvert/extrovert characteristic covers the beginning, middle and end of that spectrum. They have all proved that leadership, whether it's at summer camp or in their early career, is not based on their innate temperament.

For example, Sam is a naturally born extrovert and has always stepped up to lead, whether it be a home project, scouts or a law school project. Tucker is probably right in the middle of the introvert/extrovert spectrum and has become a leader in his early career. Joe is a naturally born introvert. He has stepped in as a leader at the family camp we attended each summer when he became a camp counselor in his college years and is always the leader of all things fantasy football. They are young still, so will see how it plays out, but what we know, and what this demonstrates, is that strong leadership does not require a dynamic approach. Of course, research supports this as well. If you need a great read to support this, start with Susan Cain's book, *Quiet*—it is outstanding!

It is helpful to know that approximately 77 percent of the population in America fall somewhere between the two extremes, including 12 percent being highly extroverted and 5 percent being highly introverted.[25]

Energy is an invisible force, yet you can feel it reverberate through the halls. When someone with high energy comes through, they raise the entire vibe.

---

25 (American Trends Panel study (HIGH5 & Review Team, August, 2024)

"Energy is the spark that gets things moving. It's the enthusiasm and passion that leaders bring to the table, and it has a contagious effect. When leaders are energetic, their teams are more INSPIRED, ENGAGED and COMMITTED."

—Colette Heneghan, MD (Company Doctor podcast)

High energy can help the team overcome stagnation, and inspire creativity and self-confidence—as well as develop resilience in times of stress. It's the combination of listening and the other areas we have covered together that with energy develop a team of excellence. I often tell the team, "If you are having a hard day, let someone know and take the time you need, but for the benefit of the team, and important work we are committed to, don't bring negative energy into the morning huddle." If it's you, the leader, having the bad day, passing off the role for that meeting is the best action you can take in that circumstance. We all have days where we can't quite bring our best energy. Recognizing this is the best thing we can do. Make a commitment to keep your energy high!

Power Theme #7: They give them the tools they need to contribute at their highest level.

This is SO important. The modern world often results in leaders and organizations that are beyond busy and are actively going after multiple goals at one time. The result is that we forget that the team needs core tools. We take for granted that everyone knows how to use the internal communication and analytic tools, such as Outlook, Teams, Slack, Salesforce, Tableau, Power BI, etc. There will be times when your team needs to know basic Human Resource policies, such as the bereavement leave policy for your organization.

When new team members join the team, they typically go through some sort of onboarding process. But they also need to get their "reps" in on some tools in order to activate the learning. What I have learned most recently in my career is that onboarding must be well thought out. I'm always actively working through ways to consider new tools, such as micro-learning video modules and reimagined mentoring, to ensure we get this right. Be sure to ask in your one-on-ones if they have what they need to do their job, and even give them examples such as Outlook meeting calendars so that they aren't embarrassed with something that may seem so basic.

A few years ago, we realized our first level managers were not doing so great at meeting management as a result of our standard employee feedback process. As we dove in more, we learned that they never had training on facilitating a good meeting. I had taken that for granted because I started my career with Sprint (now T-Mobile) and they provided a lot of training on core skills such as leading meetings for first time managers. Their process was a great example of excellence in leadership training and ensuring your team is equipped.

The Big 3 (In Summary)

- **Culture should be your first focus and number one priority.**
- **Study great coaches and leaders in another space to find someone who best aligns with your style.**
- **Know the "Power 7" when it comes to building your skills around culture and team:**

"The simplest acts of
kindness are by far more
powerful than a thousand
heads bowing in prayer."

—Mahatma Ghandi

Chapter 6

Payers Masterclass #2: The Nemesis We Need to Learn to Love

"Healthcare payers are not just financial intermediaries; they are essential partners in driving better health outcomes, ensuring access to care, and shaping a more sustainable healthcare system."

—Author unknown... but it's really spot on!

The common chapter about payers would be to highlight the different types of payers to include government, commercial or private health plans at a minimum. I am taking a different angle as I've attempted to throughout the book to instead focus on putting that book knowledge into a narrative that will help you as you launch into your career. The simple math on a typical payer market distribution generally goes something like this….

National average of payor mix

(As of 2024)

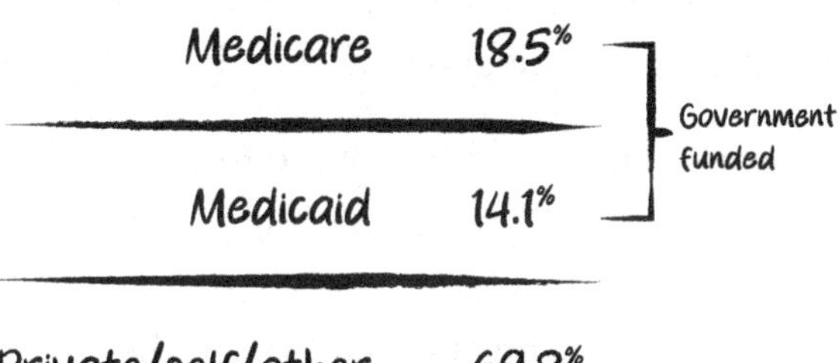

Source: Definitive Healthcare

Two Opposing Goals Drive the Tension

When I was the Chief Executive Officer in Kansas City for a large privately owned practice, I knew after about 8 years that I was ready to step into a larger role or organization. At the time, I explored many industries, including pharmaceuticals, life sciences, aligned community healthcare adjacent non-profits, and hospitals—but definitely not… payers.

Why not? As the leader of our practice, I enjoyed working with my peers at our top payers, but it was always a challenge. Claims denials, negotiating rates, prior authorization processes, etc., were all the parts of the job that I didn't love. My team of nurses, medical assistants and physicians were especially exasperated at the time it took to get their patients "through the system." Fortunately, I was able to sit on an advisory council that Blue Cross and Blue Shield of Kansas City launched to help build bridges with practice leaders of some of the largest groups throughout the city. That experience helped me understand at a very basic level how much they WANT to partner with the physician community. In fact, their business depends on having a strong network of providers who can deliver high-quality care to their shared members. There is nothing better than where there is a want and a need to drive innovation.

The initial economics are important to understand. Both the payer and the provider have different objectives in play. The provider needs to ensure their patients receive needed care, and the payer needs to control spend where they can in order to ensure financial sustainability by maintaining affordable premiums. This foundational contrast creates a challenge upfront. It seems with this as the backdrop that any alignment is unlikely. But not only is it possible—it is essential that we partner together to achieve optimal health for our communities. Healthcare leaders must understand both the nuances and the big picture and make a commitment to building strong alliances with the payer partners that span our communities.

Changing the Game and Creating Better Allies

There have a been a few key industry pivots that have played a helpful role in establishing stronger partnership. With the advent of Patient-Centered Medical Home (PCMH) in 2007, the healthcare world experienced their first contemporary framework.

PCMH is composed of the 7 principles identified below. These would essentially "set the table" for Value-Based Care (VBC) as we know it today. (We will dive deep into VBC in Chapter 10.) The most important part is it gave healthcare provider groups and payers a common starting place from which to evolve our current system.

The 7 Principles of Patient-Centered Medical Home (PCMH)

1. **Personal physician**
   Each patient has an ongoing relationship with a **personal physician** trained to provide first contact, continuous and comprehensive care.

2. **Physician directed medical practice**
   The **personal physician leads a team of individuals** at the practice level who collectively take responsibility for the ongoing care of patients.

3. **Whole person orientation**
   The personal physician is responsible for providing for **all the patient's healthcare needs** or taking responsibility for appropriately arranging care with other qualified professionals.

4. **Coordinated care**
   Care is coordinated and/or integrated across all elements of the complex healthcare system (e.g., specialty care, hospitals, home health agencies, nursing homes) and the patient's community (e.g., family, public and private community-based services).

5. **High-quality care**
   A focus on **quality and safety** are hallmarks of the medical home.

6. **Enhanced access**
   Enhanced access to care is available through systems such as open scheduling, expanded hours and new options for communication between patients, their personal physician, and practice staff.

7. **Appropriate pricing**
   Payment appropriately recognizes the added value provided to patients who have a patient-centered medical home.[26]

The great news is that this generation of payers began the work of exploring how they could best partner with the medical teams who are on the front lines providing care to ensure their members were receiving the highest quality of care, and in a manner that was sustainable and affordable. The PCMH model is one that can hardly be argued with, as it set a standard for care being quarterbacked by the primary care physician (the least expensive of the physician specialties) in a model that promises better quality and lower costs.

Most of us are aware of the high cost of medical care and how the cost of premiums grows every year. The reality is that healthcare costs are often the single highest expense for employers outside of salaries. What's happening today is employers have their employees share in the cost via payroll deductions.

When you follow the money and really understand the value chain for the payer and the other key parties, you will quickly see that the payer community should be our best ally when it comes to creating innovation and excellence for our communities. We need their strength in running the back engines of financing healthcare and partnering with employers. They risk financial exposure if the medical community and the community (the people) don't rally together to achieve both excellence in outcomes and excellence in controlling runaway expenses.

---

26 https://www.ncbi.nlm.nih.gov/pmc/articles/PMC6139911/

A terrific story to share... Blue Cross and Blue Shield of Kansas City was so ahead of the curve that they partnered with TransforMED, a non-profit subsidiary of the American Academy of Family Physicians, to provide infrastructure support to local KC medical groups as they launched PCMH. It was an incredible gift to the practices and now that I know much more, it was a brilliant move as it helped the doctors become educated and able to advance the shared goal of achieving excellence for their common customer, the patient.

> **Fun Fact:** "The Blues" (Blue Cross and Blue Shield) are almost always the local payer leader. They are closest to the communities they serve due to their national infrastructure of being run individually by states and large metropolitan communities versus being a national organization such as UHC, Aetna, and Cigna.

The Payer as an Incredible Partner

As you learn about the payers, I hope you will see them as an incredibly valuable partner. Beyond offering infrastructure support if needed, payers play a key role in our collective effort to help manage our healthcare systems.

I've listed below a few key areas you should be aware of. As you advance your career, I am hopeful that this type of list begins to expand your imagination of the many areas where we need your leadership.

Areas of Collaboration to Consider When Partnering with Payers

1. **Designing healthcare plans and products** that provide the patient access to preventive care, offering incentives and gamification in many cases to advance community health.
2. **Keeping an eye on complex pharmaceutical prescriptions** for those with chronic diseases, ensuring safety and optimizing when possible.
3. **Providing care management services with trained Registered Nurses and appropriately certified professionals** in areas such as behavioral health to help augment support for the advanced community practices but also providing critical services for those in rural communities without ready access to this level of care.

As I shared at the beginning of many Greater Kansas City Chamber Health Council meetings, "Imagine what we can accomplish if we all throw our hats in the center of the table and focus on the common good for the patient and community instead of our own agendas." The healthcare leaders around the table nodded in agreement. I believe we can only optimize our system with a strong understanding, appreciation and commitment to build relationships with our payer partners across our regions.

Embracing the Payer-Provider-Relationship Creates Lasting Change for All of Us

Cheers to all of the payers out there who are helping us all in so many ways. We have a long way to go and a lot of innovation to uncover, but we need to be at the table together solving for the best ideas to our biggest challenges.

As we move into the conversation around providers (I consider myself a Care Delivery Leader on the "provider" side of the equation, so this will be fun), you will see that the payers have their work cut out for them as the simplicity of the private physician solopreneur or group is no longer the majority, and there are now many flavors of providers that require their (and our) understanding and attention.

The Big 3 (In Summary)

- **A healthcare leader should know the major payer groups, the payer mix in our country, in their organization and, most importantly, understand the business and financial goals of the payers they partner with.**
- **Learn about the common drivers, such as PCMH, VBC, and ACA, as you think through the healthcare ecosystem and be sure to understand the payer role (why they care in each scenario). Identify the specific common goals of the payers, providers and patients.**
- **Focus on what infrastructure strategies can be put together no matter what side of the fence you sit on in order to have a starting point for best-in-class healthcare in America.**

"Strengths lie in differences,
not in similarities."

—Stephen R. Covey

Chapter 7

Providers Masterclass #3: The Ultimate Quarterbacks of Care

"A quarterback's job is to lead, to get his team in the end zone, and to win games."

—Peyton Manning- Considered one of the greatest quarterbacks in NFL history

My career started with leadership roles in two private practice organizations, initially with an OB-GYN group and then I was on to the large multi-specialty group I mentioned. These experiences both shaped me and helped me develop a deeper understanding of both my role and this incredible profession. I cherish both the learning and the people I had the honor of working with, and I honestly count these experiences as the highlight of my career so far. I loved the entrepreneurial feel of the organizations and their passion for providing such great care and running their practices in a way that gave them pride of ownership. The care factor was often "next level."

For some of you, this may call up images of Norman Rockwell paintings, which depict the nostalgia of the basic house call—and it should. It looked like waiting until 7 pm at times so a patient could get the care they needed after work, or a Saturday morning office call to ensure someone's loved one could be cared for and seek needed relief outside of the emergency room.

I began to learn that being a shareholder of a practice like this had enormous responsibility. The reward for this was that as a provider you could make your own decisions on many things, including your schedule, if you wanted a big or small office, who you hired, and to some degree, how much money you would make. Private practices can still thrive with the support of exceptional business leaders (and a strong board of directors) because at every corner, there is a need for next-level conversations on reimbursement, strategic partnerships (with laboratories, specialist/referral partners, pharmaceuticals, etc.), and negotiations of all manner (supply costs, building leases, etc.).

Sadly, for most, the cost of private practice has become unreasonable due to investments needed in infrastructure and technology, as well as the increasing complexity of human resources and compliance and risk issues. According to a January 2024 American Medical Association (AMA) study, overall private practice clinics have fallen from 60.1% to 46.7% from 2012 to 2022. For family physicians, that has dropped to 32% according to the same study.

I was surprised it was that high, honestly. I thought it was down to single digits. This topic points to the need for healthcare leaders to have a broad understanding of the overall dynamics and the providers that compose our healthcare systems. The great news is that the industry is endlessly changing with new ways for providers to engage in the overall ecosystem, which means there are the enormous of opportunities for new leaders like you to step in and ensure excellence.[27]

Did you know that the provider shortage in America is changing our entire landscape? Much like the promises or fears of global warming, the voices started at a low volume shout about 10 years ago and the volume is currently being turned up as we begin to see this reality in our day-to-day lives. This shows up as multi-week waits for an annual physical in many areas and the proliferation of virtual care options hoping to provide more services with less time.

Primary Care

In my role as the leader for a private practice, a part of our strategy for recruitment was to partner with the local medical schools. I often had the opportunity to speak to student residents about their differing opportunities when they graduated. Of course, our hope was that they'd choose to stay local with our group. I was surprised to find that most didn't really know what their options included, and many shared that they would likely work for a hospital system or in a hospital. This makes sense of course as that is where their training generally was. All in, it's not that surprising as I also had no real idea what my options were when I got started, only that I needed to make money—and hopefully

27 https://www.ama-assn.org/press-center/press-releases/ama-examines-decade-change-physician-practice-ownership-and

fast! I suspect most providers have the same primary goal: get through training and then think through the details of where they will use their new skills.

At that time, for the family or internal medicine physician, the likely choices were to join a private practice, join a hospital-owned group, or to become a hospitalist. It was simple overall, because generally your personality and tolerance for risk helped make the decision that was best for you. Those were the good ole' days. The pace of the industry is changing so quickly that it's difficult to find solid information that gives new providers material information in order to decide.

Opportunities have expanded greatly for graduates today as we see new entities, such as the payer/provider organizations, and new innovative companies, such as those I highlighted above that are actively seeking primary care providers.

See the chart below for a list of some of the many opportunities available for providers today. The goal here is to shine a light on the importance of understanding the larger environment. It's also to ensure that you have a clear understanding of the multiple avenues of where you might find your leadership skills used and best aligned with your personal goals. It's an exciting time to be in the profession!

Primary Care Options—*For Now*

- Independent (direct primary care, concierge care such as MDVIP) or traditional private practice
- Health system/hospital owned (Mayo, Cleveland, Geisinger, your local systems)

- Organization owned (for example, Oak Street is owned by CVS, Iora is owned by Amazon)
- Private equity groups (for example, VillageMD is backed by Walgreens and KKR, and Agilon Health is backed by Clayton, Dubilier and Rice [CD&R])
- Payer (Kaiser, UHC [Optum], Elevance/Anthem [CareMore], Humana [Conviva/Centerwell], BCBS [Kinwell, Prosano, Spira Care], Geisinger, etc.)
- Government supported organizations include Community health centers (these are non-profits also known as FQHCs), The Veterans Health Administration (VHA) facilities and others.

Outside of Primary Care

Of course, some of the organizations above will also be hiring **specialist physicians.** Many of the senior-focused care centers like to engage a cardiologist and other specific specialists that are often more needed in these populations such as podiatry.[28] As I shared, there are far more privately owned specialty practices, but even that is changing. For the topic of specialists, I wanted to ensure we were on the same page with the most common. These include those in:

- Cardiology
- Oncology
- Hematology
- Infectious Diseases
- Ear, Nose and Throat (ENT)

28 ChenMed is a great example of this.

- Neurology
- Psychiatry
- Plastic Surgery
- Obstetrics and gynecology
- Gastroenterology
- Urology
- Dermatology
- General Surgery
- Emergency Medicine
- Anesthesiology
- Radiology
- Orthopedics
- Rheumatology
- Endocrinology

One thing to watch as we continue to see the shortage in physicians and providers across America and the aging of our population is that the competition for their talent is heating up.

Fun Fact: Today, we have specialty providers engaged by private equity (PE) firms hoping to get a stake in the game. When we get to the Value-Based Care (VBC) chapter, you will see that VBC's enablement organizations, Privia and Astrana Care Partners, are building infrastructure and momentum around specialty organizations which will truly be needed to lower the overall cost of care.

Other than specialists, there are other providers to think about when you consider the overall category. Think about *where* they are needed across the entire healthcare ecosystem. Below you'll find a general rundown of some of the larger categories of care to understand:

- Urgent Care focused organizations (Minute Clinic, for example, is part of CVS Health, with Amwell providing telehealth services mainly for members of large payers.)
- Skilled Nursing (Rehab focused)
- Long-Term Care
- Home Health (multiple approaches from daily care to more extensive support)
- Allied Professionals such as Physical Therapy (PT), Occupational Therapy (OT), Speech Pathology
- Hospice Care
- Health System/Hospitals
- Ambulatory Surgery Centers (ASCS) providing an alternate site of service for basic surgeries
- Infusion Centers providing an alternate site of service for high-cost infusions
- Diagnostic Imaging providing an alternate site of service for expensive imaging
- Laboratories
- Pharmacies
- Employer clinics, operated by organizations such as Crossover and Premise
- Behavioral Health

There are also so many others from adjacent entities like Dental, Chiropractic, and Optometry.

"Next-Level" Providers

Organizations such as Galileo, founded by Tom Lee, M.D., will certainly be one of many players as our country unfolds. Galileo has the goal to be your health partner 24/7 with mobile access to a care team, supporting primary care and chronic condition management. They no doubt will continue to break barriers and reach rural markets and others as we all become more accustomed to the value that can be found in mobile medicine.

Many providers are using services such as "bedside consultations" with companies like PicassoMD or RubaconMD. These services provide the primary care provider with the ability to consult with board-certified specialists and support them during their visit to explore whether a specialty referral is needed, or if there is another way to solve for their current issue with the support of on-call specialists. To bring this to life, here is a real life experience that was shared recently. The primary care group had a 12-year-old patient that came in for an upper respiratory condition. At the visit, he shared that he had a rash on his arm. The primary care doctor was able to reach out to a dermatologist during the visit and rule out anything serious. This removed frustration for his mother, who would have had to schedule another visit, pay another copay and take time off work. This also saved him the time he would have missed from school. Another example was a 40-year old man who was getting ready to leave the next day on a long-planned family trip to Mexico. He began experiencing what felt like a kidney stone and called on his primary care doctor. She was able to consult with a urologst from the exam room, who quickly expedited a sonogram and was able to give him care instructions that enabled him to address the pain, go on the trip and deal with the necessary follow up upon his return. In this case, the ability to navigate the experience for the patient in a short time frame couldn't have been done without this innovation. Needless, to say, both patients were thrilled with the overall experience, and the cost to our healthcare system was less than what is normally the case for similar situations.

There are so many powerful stories demonstrating ways this approach has accomplished the goals of delivering for the patient an exceptional experience and reducing the costs of overall healthcare for all involved. This is a great example of how the industry is rethinking antiquated models of care and bringing true value to our health system and to our communities! Win. Win.

Federally Qualified Health Center (FQHC) Providers and the Veteran's Administration (VA): A Special Call-Out

Let's spend a bit more time with two powerful parts of our healthcare ecosystem: our country's FQHC and VA care organizations. Both are found in almost every city in across America, and they play a key role in offering primary care, as well as pharmacy, dental and mental health services for those that often need it the most. This is especially important, because it requires an entirely different infrastructure than the traditional provider model, due to its primary paying customer being the government (the taxpayer).

Fun Fact: Federally Qualified Health Centers were expected to serve 34 million, or 1 out of 11 Americans, in 2024 according to Definitive Healthcare.[29]

The Department of Veterans Affairs (aka the "VA") is set to serve another $9M.[30]

The need for innovation is perhaps most greatly needed in this space. You may have heard the term "Community Health Workers." In the FQHC universe, these associates are employed with a primary goal of helping patients navigate their health while addressing the social determinants of health, providing health education and connecting patients with community resources. This can play out in many ways, but one example is Asian Health Services in Oakland, California.

Their ability to help address language barriers is a clear example of how we can improve the health of our communities. Another great example is how FQHCs often use team-based chronic disease management programs to address the realities of chronic disease and get to better outcomes with a multi-strategy approach, including education, group visits and outcomes tracking.

As for the VA, other than a few family members who have shared their experiences over the years, I had a physician partner, Dr. Ahmed, who raised my awareness of the important work happening within the Veterans Administration. In their Patient-Aligned Care Teams (PACT) model, the patient is assigned to a dedicated care team. This team has the goal of

29 https://www.definitivehc.com
30 https://www.va.gov

providing comprehensive care and many have seen impressive results, like increased satisfaction, less emergency visits and an increase in the quality of care.[31]

Additionally, we think of Covid as having driven the rest of the industry to finally adopt telehealth widely. The VA has been a true pioneer in this area and has focused their efforts here on behalf of rural veterans, through their use of what they refer to as "VA Video Connect," a virtual care platform allowing veterans to access services remotely. There are many other examples, and I hope that you will take the time to understand what is happening in these important provider spaces as you examine the overall ecosystem and your opportunities.

And Now for the Payer/Provider Combo

As you can see, there are multiple provider opportunities, and more are being added each year. I hope this information is helpful as you explore what areas align best with your heart and soul.

The next chapter on the payer/provider combined organizations is certainly worth your attention. It's exciting to watch as their synergies seem to be just what our country might need to advance our work.

31 https://www.hsrd.research.va.gov/research/citations/pubbriefs/articles.cfm?RecordID=665

The Big 3 (In Summary)

- Primary care is the key provider to understand. In most models of care, they are the quarterback and have the ability to control the total cost of care based on how they navigate the patient through the healthcare system.
- Other provider examples seem to be endless as we think about the span from birth to the end of life. It's fun to consider the MANY faces of providers and how we might intersect as leaders on behalf of the patients we serve.
- Be sure to explore what is happening for unique populations. Plato's famous quote, "Necessity is the mother of invention" seems to hold true. You will find that much of our healthcare innovation is found in areas that need it most, such as we found out during the the Covid pandemic.

"It's not enough to be busy. So are the ants. The question is, what are we busy about?"

—Henry David Thoreau

Chapter 8

Payer and Provider Partnerships Masterclass #4: Leveraging Strengths to Help Solve Our Biggest Problems

"The people who are crazy enough to think they can change the world are the ones who do."

—Rob Siltanen-creator of Apple's Think Different campaign

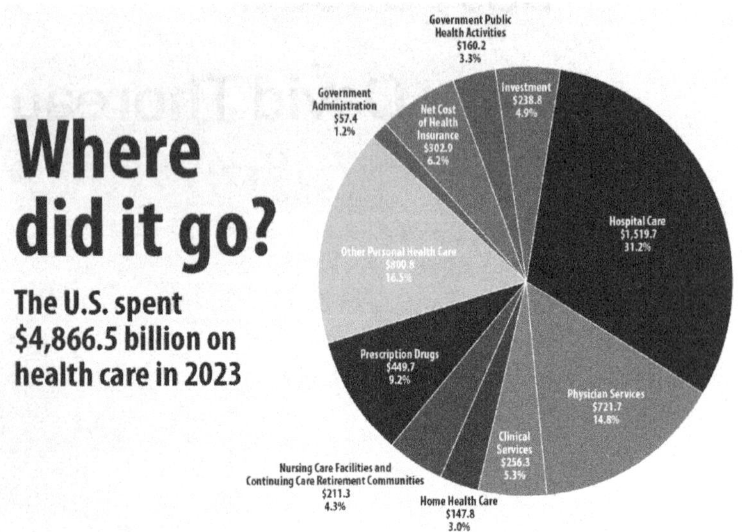

https://www.ama-assn.org/about/research/trends-health-care-spending

This chapter has the goal of building on Part 1 by expanding your knowledge of how the payer and the provider (also considered the two primary players) are coming together to solve our biggest challenges. As you can see in the visual above, we have a long way to go as a country despite many efforts. **To put it simply, the goal is for two forward thinking parties to come together in a meaningful way in order to improve our health systems.** At the core of this is creating progress based on shared goals and aligned incentives. Payer-provider partnerships can be carried out in many ways the Blue Cross and Blue Shield organizations in Kansas, Missouri, Washington and Arizona models currently in play.[32] Often, we will see two different parties come together to create synergies and address community needs such as the Banner Health and Aetna partnership.[33]

> **Pro Tip:** Using cross-industry examination to explore and ideate healthcare strategy has always proven to be a game-changer for me in all of my healthcare roles. Using ideas from the grocery or automotive industries for example can be powerful. (It's awesome!)

At times, these partnerships become an acquisition, such as CVS Health and Aetna, as shared in the box below. As we ignite the conversation, I want you to think about the significance of these examples, including the two outside of the healthcare industry.

---

32 I am a huge fan of vertical integrations—although they are complex and require the highest level of communication, leadership and resources throughout the entire system for success to be achieved.

33 https://www.banneraetna.com/

Strategic Partnerships and Their Goals

2017, Amazon & Whole Foods

Make high quality, organic food more affordable and accessible for everyone.[34]

2018, CVS Health & Aetna

Provide consumers with a better experience (i.e., quality), reduced costs and improved access to healthcare

2021, T Mobile & Sprint

Expand the network, and combine resources to bring coverage (i.e., access), service (i.e., quality) and value (i.e., affordability) to customers.

In all of these cases, while the consumer or patient is at the center, there are three consistent driving strategies at play:

1. **Improve Quality**
2. **Improve Access**
3. **Improve Affordability**

These of course should be familiar as they are also key drivers rooted in the Patient Centered Medical Home models, and all of Value-Based Care. Honestly, if you distill down most partnerships, regardless of industry, these three, along with growth, seem to be universal.

34 (CNBC.com 8/2022)

Examples of Payer-Provider Partnerships

Vertical Integration (The payer and provider are one in the same)

The first is Kaiser Permanente, which was founded in California in 1945. They now cover ten states. When I started studying their history, I thought about how much and what little has changed over the past 8 decades. I imagine their founders felt the same way at the conclusion of their careers. The famous Kaiser model integrates the payer and provider under one model. A few different business structures exist to create their overall ecosystem.[35]

Their goal is to provide a "one-stop shop" experience so that patients don't have to navigate multiple waters to get their healthcare needs taken care of. In many areas of the country, this includes having the hospital, medical providers and the insurance/financial part all under the same organizational experience. (Organizations are typically the payer and provider but not the hospital.) This type of streamlining has so many benefits, and my experience at BCBSAZ demonstrated that you can truly create something special when the power of the payer and provider come together.

The Kaiser story is fascinating. The takeaway here is that their model has been an evolving integrated model for many years, and most would say with wild success based on their financial trajectory and expansion. Their growth makes you wonder why traction in this type of model hasn't been the most common.

---

35 https://en.wikipedia.org/wiki/Kaiser_Permanente

Kaiser continues to take ground and in fact recently founded Risant Health in 2023, which is a nonprofit organization formed to create a national Value-Based Care network. Over the last year, closing in April of 2024, Risant recently acquired the highly regarded Geisinger health system in Pennsylvania. This move gave them a strong foundation of 10 hospitals with which to begin their goal of partnership expansion as they solve for achieving Value-Based Care across their patient base. Kaiser and Risant are definitely a vertical integration to watch. You could say they are pioneering innovative approaches to solve for better healthcare—at scale and much faster than has been experienced in our country.

Joint Ventures

Accountable Care Organizations (ACOs) were a product of the Accountable Care Act (ACA), which was signed into law in 2010, and the Medicare Shared Savings Program (MSSP), which launched in 2012. Once again, the **goals were to get to improved quality and cost**. The healthcare system would do this through the common levers of improved care coordination and chronic condition management while expanding on gaining provider engagement in the ground game via paying incentives to support their time and attention.

Building on PCMH's improvement and incentive programs, ACOs bring providers together. The common goal is establishing leadership and operational systems that help them accelerate their performance and, together with their peers, produce collective results.

One major outcome here has been that some of these have brought forward partnerships that are continuing to grow and expand. One such example is Banner Health and Aetna. Banner Health is headquartered in Phoenix, Arizona, and is one of the largest, nonprofit healthcare systems and providers in the country, serving a total of six states.[36]

What started as an ACO has turned into a joint venture (JV) worth studying. The Banner/Aetna JV is an affiliate of both separate companies by structure, and together they formed an organization in 2017 that brings together the strengths of both organizations to enhance care coordination and improve outcomes. Their co-branded health insurance product uses Banner's network and Aetna's insurance expertise to offer consumers a focused choice committed to Value-Based Care with aligned partners.

Strategic Alliances

There are so many strategic alliances, it is challenging to select one for illustration. Strategic alliances are the easiest (due to legal and operational issues mainly) way to embark on a partnership when bringing together two entities. Questions for a leader to ask might be:

- **"Who does this aspect of healthcare better than us, and can they help us meet our (shared) goals?"**
- **"Who is aligned with our mission and culture?"**
- **"Who is someone we would be proud to be aligned with?"**

36 https://www.bannerhealth.com

Fun Fact: One of America's stalwart organizations, the Cleveland Clinic, partnered with a rather new health plan entrant, Oscar Health. Oscar is a self-proclaimed "technology-driven insurance platform."

Oscar recently hired former CEO of Aetna, Mark Bertolini, as their Chief Executive Officer, which makes this far more interesting. This partnership is one to watch! Oscar and Cleveland came together in 2018. They shared a goal to offer a co-branded health insurance plan product in Ohio. They started in a small area in the Northeastern part of the state, specifically for the Individual market, or what we know as the ACA or Health Insurance Marketplace.

Oscar's tech-enabled platform offers features such as 24/7 telemedicine and the use of "smart health data" to improve care management. Cleveland Clinic's brand name and excellent reputation have been leveraged so that consumers now have access to the Oscar/Cleveland partnership through their employer as well as the Marketplace. This is a great example of a strategic alliance where both parties appear to be focused on continued innovation and achieving success together.

These are the payer-provider partnerships that are most talked about in the industry, but so many more exist, often with little fanfare. In my personal experience I have been a part of many partnerships with payers, including everything from basic infrastructure support, such as together accelerating care coordination programs, to larger efforts to help grow our patient base by introducing a new health plan product aimed at providing better care and access to meet a specific community need.

These payer-provider partnerships are especially helpful when health plans build out narrow networks or other special networks to meet a patient demographic need. From a payer perspective, I have seen many small joint ventures with local medical groups who shared a common goal to expand or grow in an area, or to attack the high cost of a specific demographic.

I hope you are beginning to see the importance of understanding the key parties individually and the power of what could be when you bring them together to help us achieve "better" in American Healthcare. **I truly believe that we can achieve excellence, and I will always believe partnership is the best path for that to happen.**

This is the perfect time to jump into the VBC World. As we move on to one of my favorite topics, we will continue to build on partnerships, as well as discuss why in the world investors would be so interested in the VBC aspect of healthcare.

VBC has had a tough reputation at times, and for good reason, as it's often talked about broadly without noting hard evidence that it can truly be both successful and scaled widely. There is, in other words, a lot of talk and not a lot of widespread true results to show for all of the effort and attention, outside of the Medicare population.

My professional opinion is that we have only scratched the surface. We have so much to learn from the Medicare and Medicaid spaces that have been ahead of the curve here. The future is bright for VBC to truly help us get to financially responsible outcomes—and more importantly getting to the best care for our populations.

The Big 3 (In Summary)

- Most partnerships (and programs) are rooted in the common themes of improved quality, improved access and delivering on affordability. Start there when working on potential partnerships.
- Payers and providers often have shared goals. If there is a way to partner in your community, it is worthy of your time and attention.
- Explore your local or regional ACOs or similar entities. Don't be afraid to consider deeper relationship options such as strategic alliances or joint ventures.

“And, above all, be willing to learn from anyone and everyone, regardless of their station in life.”

—Ryan Holiday

Chapter 9

Value-Based Care Masterclass #5: The Essential Topic

"Value-based care is not a trend. It is the foundation of a sustainable, patient-centered healthcare system that we can all be proud of."

—Author Unknown....but I wish it was mine.

The aim of this book is to help those who desire to be leaders in the healthcare industry better understand what is going on in the day-to-day life of an actual healthcare leader. As a healthcare executive, on both the payer and provider sides of the business, Value-Based Care (VBC) drives much of the work in one way or the other. Therefore, it is essential that team members are not only knowledgeable but also feel prepared to jump into critical conversations around the role VBC plays in their role or organization.

All Americans ought to understand the basic concepts of what true Value-Based Care is and be able to assess if their healthcare providers are actively working toward achieving care at the highest quality and most sustainable cost. It is a bit perplexing that with health at the center of our existence, more time is spent discussing global warming. (No shade to global warming, but you get the point.) I'd love the conversation around the dinner table to turn to, "What are we doing specifically to ensure a strong and viable healthcare system for future generations?"

Unfortunately, when I have asked many newly minted master's in healthcare administration interviewees to "Tell me about Value-Based Care," much of the time, they cannot answer the question to any degree that illustrates a clear understanding. Often, the answer is something like, "Is that when a doctor spends more time with the patient (thus providing more value-)?"

This is not a criticism of the university programs, but of the truth that almost all of us learn firsthand or through stories. That said, my goal is to frame the concept in a way that helps us get to a clearer portrayal of how Value-Based Care plays out in today's healthcare world. It is my belief that transforming healthcare depends on us all accelerating knowledge and creating strategies with Value-Based Care as the central infrastructure.

Rewiring Our Healthcare System

I am not certain why the idea of "rewiring" came to mind as I ideated around how to best get to the topic of Value-Based Care, but when I did a bit of research on rewiring a home, I immediately got my answer:

"While rewiring may seem like a major ***investment****, it* ***reduces your risk*** *of experiencing a house fire,* ***increases the value*** *of your home,* ***improves the safety*** *of your home,* ***saves you money*** *on electrical bills, and* ***increases*** *your home's electrical* ***capacity****."*

It's perfect really…

The following six areas are what we will explore in this mini masterclass after we level set on the most common "need to know" parts of a Value-Based agreement.[37]

6 Truths of Value-Based Care

1. Value-Based Care is a major investment.
Large financial investments in technology, people, education and resources are required to modify the current care delivery system, which is centered on a fee for service methodology versus payment for value.

2. Value-Based Care reduces risk.
Perhaps the most significant promise of Value-Based Care is improving healthcare quality.

3. Value-Based Care increases value.
VBC increases the value of the care we receive.

4. Value-Based Care improves safety.
With investments in technology, there is a far greater opportunity to reduce healthcare errors.

5. Value-Based Care saves money.
The goal of VBC is to create a more financially viable healthcare system, while improving quality.

6. Value-Based Care increases capacity.
VBC has the opportunity to drive healthcare services to the best provider, while removing the current complexities of the old system, thereby allowing us to better take care of our nation's people.

37 There is also The National Academy of Medicine's description of VBC which is STEEP: Safe, Timely, Effective, Efficient, Equitable, Patient Centered.

Foundational Elements

Is There a Universal Language I Need to Be Aware Of?

When thinking through Value-Based Care, there are a few key terms to learn and understand. Since I have been in the industry since the inception of VBC, I will say that in no way did the education I have or the conferences I attended cover many of these concepts. I had to learn them on the ground. I am especially thankful for my time spent at Humana, where I learned most of this. This was due to their focus on our nation's seniors and serving as a national leader in transforming payment and care practices to best care for this growing population. The concepts that build a VBC model are used in contracts between providers and payers. They are the topics driving the business in the conference rooms and board rooms for anyone on the care delivery side of the healthcare system.

Here is what you need to know...

The Spectrum of Value-Based Care Categories

This is an important one, and foundational to our VBC conversation. There is a known "Alternative Payment Model" also known as the **"APM Framework,"** which was developed by the **Health Care Payment Learning and Action Network, or LAN,** in 2016 to drive alignment in payment approaches across the public and private sectors of the US healthcare system.[38]

---

38 According to HCPLAN: "The APM Framework is the HCPLAN's landmark achievement, establishing a common vocabulary and pathway for measuring successful payment models. Originally published in 2016 and refreshed in 2017, the Framework classifies Alternative Payment Models (APMs) in four categories and eight subcategories, specifying decision rules to standardize classification efforts. It lays out core principles for designing APMs, which have influenced payers and purchasers, and forms the basis of the annual Measurement Effort".

As you will see below, there are 4 major categories, with Category 1 being a Fee for Service only model with no payment or reimbursement to providers of healthcare systems for quality or value of care delivered. The optimum step is Category 4, where it is a full "population-based payment," meaning the provider is at what we refer to as "full risk." In other words, the payer gives the provider (or provider representative, such as an ACO), a set amount to take care of the patient, and they do so by meeting or exceeding minimum thresholds of quality and value and take the risk if they do not. If they can deliver excellent care and keep the spending in check, they will reap the reward, and their patients will be better for it.

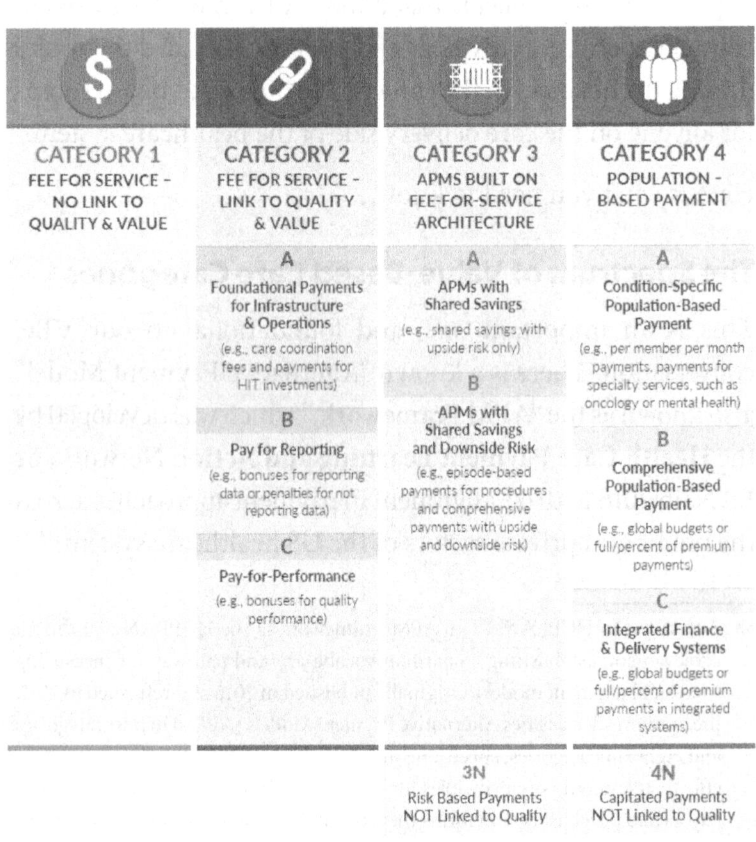

Let's Get Clear on the Language

MLR (Medical Loss Ratio)

There is typically a targeted "medical loss ration" or "MLR" goal in a VBC agreement or contract. What this means is that based on some type of valuation (typically driven by recent historical results) by the actuarial teams, a percent is identified as the expected "medical loss" for the contract period. For example, for every $1 of premium, the plan may expect an 88 percent MLR. The remaining money is for administration costs. Providers in the VBC contracts have the goal of meeting or beating this expected cost of care.

Quality Targets

Quality is determined by the provider's performance according to HEDIS measures (Healthcare Effectiveness Data and Information Set). This is a tool brought forth by the National Committee for Quality (NCQA) in 2001. It is used by more than 90 percent of health plans to measure performance on important dimensions of care and services and is updated annually.

HEDIS measures are collected via the provider and typically captured in their electronic medical records. The organizations pull the data from EMR datascts, and via claims and medical records systems, they ensure they have captured a full picture of these categories. HEDIS also captures a patient experience component, which is completed through a survey process.

You will also hear the term "STARS" often, which is the Center for Medicare and Medicaid Services (CMS) published STAR ratings. This system rates on a scale of 1 to 5, with 5 being the highest rate for government sponsored plans.

Performance Metrics

These are additional focus areas, which are designed to help the provider achieve success in the VBC agreement. Examples include utilization metrics, such as hospital admission and lengths of stay, re-admission rates, preventable emergency room visits and skilled nursing facility average lengths of stay. Others may include specialty spend, prescription drug costs and capturing social determinants of health (SDoH). This list will expand and change along with the trends and changes in the overall care of our population and cost trends.

Patient Attribution Methodology

All agreements are designed to cover a designated part of the "population health" for that provider's responsibility. In doing so, it is important to understand how those patients will be attributed. For example, if I go to Primary Care Physician A for 2 visits and Primary Care Physician B for 1 visit, who should my care be attributed to?

Risk Adjustment (Medicare Patients)

Medicare and Medicaid patients are reimbursed by the government on a risk adjustment methodology. This means that it is important that a provider accurately documents a patient's conditions. If a patient is more complex, such as having diabetes and a heart condition, they will be reimbursed higher to allow the provider to properly care for that complexity. Most agreements stress the importance of ensuring the provider is adequately documenting a patient's full healthcare picture so that there is enough reimbursement to pay for the expected care needed.

Care Coordination

This is a complex area. It often includes performance metrics, ensuring a high percentage of the population have had their Annual Wellness Visits. These metrics also serve to ensure that patients are followed up with after an emergency department visit or any inpatient visit and that care coordination includes medication reconciliation post-discharge, often within 30 days or less.

Investments Needed to "Rewire" Healthcare

Underscore this: VBC requires a major investment. There are two parts of this investment from my experience: one financial and one human capital (also resulting in a financial investment). As with anything foundational, the resource requirements are significant.

As a healthcare leader, being familiar with the many potential components is critical. I will say that these costs should be considered an ongoing "major investment" in the overall budget. Some of the key areas that may be required:

Electronic Medical Records: At this point, according to the National Center for Health Statistics, over 90 percent of all physicians have adopted an EMR.[39] Although the initial investment has been made, many of these have monthly software fees and all of them will have required upgrades which need to be considered in the budget.

Data Analytics or Population Health Platforms: An EMR serves as the repository, codifying thousands of important bits

39 It's hard to believe that we didn't have an EMR when I started in my career. Our physicians used to literally carry boxes of paper records out to their vehicles each night so they could document their patient visits. Incredible progress.

of information. However, most EMRS do not automatically have a robust data extraction function which will allow the leadership team to translate the data to actionable insights to truly achieve the goals of improving population health and, of course, meet the goals of the Value-Based Agreement.

There are many innovative companies beginning to demonstrate that a strong population health management tool is worth its weight in gold in creating real change. Imagine a tool that uses predictive analytics to identify high-risk patients early and provides proposed pathways to help manage these conditions and thereby improves their lives and reduces total healthcare costs! Organizations such as Matellio suggest we can expect these tools to yield a 3:1 or 5:1 return on investment.[40]

Technology Hardware Costs: This will span from having desktop, laptop or mobile devices available for all staff, including extra equipment available in case of a failure, as well as all adjacent equipment such as servers for data storage, backup systems, and facility updates to ensure Wi-Fi or a strong signal access. **The list is expansive, and my point here is to ensure you ask yourself the question, "What else?"** My IT teams have always had to sit me down and educate me on the many details and investments that were required.

Human Capital: From personal experience, I believe that a leader should at least double what they initially believe to be true in this area. This area includes all things team training and education. To expand a bit, operating a true VBC focused organization is essentially creating a new "way

---

40 Determining an ROI is an exercise that needs careful analysis and consideration by your teams—and estimates by organizations selling the product should be highly vetted. They generally are not inclusive and therefore incorrect unfortunately. (They do sound great in a presentation, though ...)

of life," in the practice. This requires retraining current staff along with building out the process. It also often requires new communication pathways for them to follow, as well as creating strong onboarding systems for new team members. Additionally, VBC often requires new roles, such as care coordinators and data analysts. It is also likely that you will require provider leadership to assist in championing the efforts across the organization. This is a cost that many do not consider and is critical for success.

Risk Management: In this area, it depends on where you are on the LAN categories above. If you are sharing risk in any way, then having a stop-loss insurance policy is needed, as well as considering new programs to manage the complex patients in your panel.

Compliance and Data Management: The higher the level of the VBC agreement, the more important it is to ensure strong talent and strong technology in this area is in place to ensure your organization is managing the requirements of the agreement successfully. These are likely added costs.

Transition Costs: As a practice takes on more "risk," they will have downtime for the clinical and non-clinical staff. If they were in a fee-for-service only world, it takes time to impact the overall value and begin to truly see that investment returned. An organization should be prepared for seeing less patients during some stages of the transition.

I realize this sounds like a lot, but there is good news. Much like rewiring a home, a lot gets better after that initial investment. Value-Based Care models have proven better healthcare can be achieved and that we can together truly reduce the cost of care in America. That alone is enough for all of us to be "heads down" until we are all comfortably and fully using these models for care delivery.

Another bit of good news: many payers will partner with organizations as they are fully aligned on achieving this same goal. The next paragraph highlights one payer's perspective.

Getting to Meaningful Progress Through Infrastructure Support

There is an exceptional Harvard study that I learned about through a UnitedHealth Group article a few years ago that highlighted a critical component to effective VBC: "**Infrastructure support.**" [41]

I have highlighted some of their work below, which I fully support and almost wanted to scream "YES, YES, YES!" as I reviewed it for the first time. I have since distributed it widely to healthcare executive leaders, and since we aren't "there" yet, I feel like all healthcare leaders should keep this as a foundational document.

The goal of the report was to better understand how VBC works by reviewing 10 years' worth of VBC programs. Their report, **"A 3D Model for Value-Based Care," identified infrastructure support as the missing third dimension that accompanies quality and spending-reduction incentives."** What this means practically is that after studying the results of actual VBC programs, the authors found that physician practices need more support to be successful in Value-Based Care. There is no doubt that most practices hope to provide the highest quality and the best price; however, the competing realities of healthcare don't allow them to always meet this

41 (unitedhealthgroup.com, 10/1/2019)

target. **If a payer (or some other related party) can provide foundational support through helping create the scaffolding necessary to build a strong program, the belief is that we can scale these programs and outcomes much more quickly.**

6 Ways to Build Infrastructure Support for a Practice

1. Analyze data or reports on spending, quality and key measures.
2. Provide technical assistance to help build new capacities such as training, knowledge sharing and learning collaboratives.
3. Produce raw, unanalyzed administrative claims-based data.
4. Make infrastructure payments in the form of in-kind financial supports not linked to performance.
5. Conduct risk management support to protect participants from large losses.
6. Offer access to care management support such as personnel or tools to assist with patient care and coordination.

In interviews with 24 leading VBC providers for the study, five themes emerged for the next generation of VBC.

1. Value-based programs require substantial organizational change.
2. Shared data is the foundation of successful VBC relationships.
3. Increased capacity in care management strengthens their practice.

4. Re-setting payer provider relationships unlocks innovative program design.
5. Leadership commitment and stamina are critical success factors.

Now, let's look at the long-term result of making these investments in Value-Based Care.

5 Benefits of Rewiring Healthcare in Favor of Value-Based Care

1. Reduced Risk

This is closely aligned with improving quality. When you have your team focused on improving objective performance metrics, such as A1C control, you improve outcomes and that not only improves the patient's life but reduces risk in the overall healthcare system due to the high cost of diabetes and the secondary and tertiary disease states that often follow these diagnoses.

2. Increased Value

Value in care or the Value Equation" states that:

Value = Quality + Service / Cost

I really liked the simplicity of this, although I have not yet used it actively. I believe this is a good way to help providers wrap their heads around the "whys" in this transformation. A focused VBC program increases value because the team is unified around providing the highest quality, capturing this data so it can be tracked. This manifests as offering the highest service to all community members (equity), and when we do this, our costs are reduced over time, creating the increased value in care. Simple, right?

3. Improved Safety

Back in 2002, I did my master's thesis on the topic of medical errors in America. This was driven by the well-regarded research article, "To Err is Human" which came out via the Institute of Medicine (IOM) just a few years prior in 1999. Right after that research was done, the Healthgrades Patient Safety in American Hospitals Study took a closer look and found that the IOM study was likely well understated.

At that time, it was felt that over 195,000 deaths each year were a result of medical errors at a cost of more than $6 billion per year. "This is equivalent to 390 jumbo jets full of people dying each year due to likely preventable, in-hospital medical errors, making this one of the leading killers in the United States," shared Dr. Samantha Collier, Healthgrades's then vice president of medical affairs. [42]

An article in February of 2024 published by the National Library of Medicine shared that the numbers haven't gotten better. They hover around the 200,000 annual deaths mark, resulting in a cost somewhere between $20-45 billion annually.[43] **The question for healthcare leaders is: "Can Value-Based Care in some way help improve this ongoing tragedy?"** The answer is, "Yes, of course." The use of advanced technology will help mitigate medication errors, as one example. Of course, VBC is not going to solve everything, but it is a tool we can and should use to improve patient safety.

42 (medicalnewstoday.com- In Hospital Deaths from Medical Errors at 195,000 per year)
43 (ncbi.nlm.nih.gov, Rodziewicz, Houseman, Vaqar, and Hipskind)

4. Reduced Costs

Medical waste is a broad topic in healthcare and some estimates have the cost of this waste at 20-25% of our total healthcare spend. Let's imagine that if our Gross Domestic Product (GDP) on health spending, which is currently at 17.3%, could be reduced to 13.05%. In his article on the topic, William Shrank, M.D., and his colleagues highlighted that this is more than the country spends on primary and secondary education for all children. Appalling.[44]

Medical waste can stem from failures in care delivery, failures in the coordination of care resulting in duplicate testing, overtreatment, pricing failures, administration complexity, fraud and abuse. Value-Based Care models offer us the opportunity to get after waste through the care coordination components in particular and models such as the advanced primary care models where the care is being quarterbacked by a primary care provider team who can help eliminate duplicate efforts, ensure proper specialty referrals and even help educate patients on the various costs based on site of service selection.[45]

5. Increased Capacity

An updated article in March of 2024 by the Association of American Colleges highlights that we will see major deficits in physicians workforce across the United States. Their estimate is a shortage of up to 86,000 by 2036. With the population growth in that same period targeted at 8.4% and the aging population (64 and older projected to grow by 34.1%), we are headed toward a national crisis. Yes, there is a lot being done to

---

44 (cms.gov,, 9/10/24 article)

45 (Waste in the US Healthcare System, Shrank, Rogstad, Parekh- 2019 – jamanetwork.com)

help mitigate this, including the increase in Advanced Practice Practitioners (Nurse Practitioners, Physician Assistants, etc.); however, innovation is required to continue to explore how we can take better care of our patients with less impact on the provider team. Advanced Value-Based Care models make good use of technology and have increasingly pivoted to remote care for basic needs and using services such as I shared above with PicassoMD or RubiconMD.[46]

Value-Based Care Has Noble Promises

As a healthcare leader, recognizing and understanding the benefits of fully investing in VBC is essential to our country's ongoing ability to provide care for our growing and aging population. To me, this is perhaps the most exciting part of our roles as leaders due to the incredibly important work that needs to be done. It's taking the best of our teams, unifying around the goal and creating pathways that just flat out make for healthier people— and that means healthier communities.

That, my friend, is something worthy. I am proud to be a part of this chapter in our country, and I know you will be as well. As we wrap up our Mini Masterclass section, we now get to explore the future. I hope the last few chapters have started to stir in you an imagination for what could be, because that is where we are headed and it's going to be fun.

46 (New AAMC Report Shows Continuing Projected Physician Shortage-aamc.org)

The Big 3 (In Summary)

- Value-Based Care is essential learning for all healthcare leaders. This is perhaps the topic (other than people leadership) that is the most critical for you to understand.
- Value-Based Care can be thought of as an entire "rewiring" of our healthcare systems.
- As a healthcare leader, you have an enormous ability to make a significant impact on the health of America. Isn't that awesome?

"Just keep swimming..."

—Dory, *Finding Nemo*

Part III

Future Scan

Chapter 10

Trends: People, Money and the Patient

"Business leaders must not only disrupt but be prepared to be disrupted, to embrace change as the only constant, and to understand that the true disruptor is always looking to the horizon, not just to the bottom line. Often exhausting yes, but that's where the need arises to work smarter and in my opinion that starts with emotional intelligence and taking customer insights and relationships to a new level of expertise."

–Kate Hardcastle MBE,
a leading consumer engagement specialist[47]

Ch-Ch-Cha-Changes (David Bowie lyric...)

We live in a world of Amazon now dropping off much of our household needs, vacationing in personal homes via Airbnb and enjoying a personal driver via Uber—or even a self-driving vehicle with Waymo. All of these conveniences come with a few simple taps of our phone. What's next?

47 https://www.businessleader.co.uk/disrupting-disruptors-lessons-adapt-change

This is a far-reaching topic and one that is quite exhilarating from my point of view. Imagining what could be and what will become is energizing. To me, the potential to be one of the world's next trailblazers is the best part of being a healthcare leader. **Our world is always needing bright minds, and good energy to solve our toughest challenges.** I'm personally hopeful you will jump into the future with both enthusiasm and expectancy.

My focus for this chapter is really to paint a picture of why you as a healthcare leader must maintain a broad view and always be a student of your career and passion. It may surprise you since you are reading this book, but sadly, it is more typical for leaders to get an initial education and only participate in required company learning experiences than it is to actively learn and grow in the industry. You are already a step ahead!

We will start illustrating the canvas by covering some larger topics that will get your "thought circuits" fired up and thinking through the categories that may interest you the most. In the theme of overall change, I think we can all literally "feel" the pace of change all around us, as if we don't expect anything to be the same for too long. I believe this is why some find it challenging or even defeating to try to keep up. Time is precious, and we simply cannot afford to follow unworthy rabbit trails.

We must, however, pursue knowledge and actively stay open to the growing conversation. I felt that this information from Accenture's Pulse of Change 2024 index report was both clear and helpful in driving home the big picture on the major consideration points:[48] The report is built on a range

48 Accenture is a global consulting powerhouse and Fortune 500 company that specializes in information technology services and management consulting.

of key business indicators such as labor productivity and IT spending and quantifies the change companies are facing across six factors: Technology, Talent, Economic, Geopolitical, Climate and Consumer & Social. It then compares this data to a survey of 3,400 C-suite executives on how they view the impact of each factor on their organizations, as well as their preparedness to respond. I share this to acknowledge the depth and credibility of the work. Their four key findings are below.

Accenture's Pulse of Change 2024 Index Report, Four Key Findings

- The rate of change affecting businesses has risen steadily since 2019, by **183% over the past four years and by 33% in the past year** alone.
- **Most C-suite executives expect the pace of change to accelerate, yet more than half admit they are not fully prepared to respond.**
- Catapulted by advances in generative AI, technology changes increased the most in 2023, rising to the No. 1 cause of change from No.6 in 2022.
- Talent, the No. 2 cause of business change, is ranked No. 4 by C-suite leaders – signifying a perception gap.[49]

As an experienced healthcare leader, this idea of the "pace" of change and the impact it has on our ability to succeed at the level we desire resonates strongly. I will say again: my

49 https://www.accenture.com/content/dam/accenture/final/accenture-com/document-2/Accenture-Pulse-of-Change-2024-Index-Executive-Summary.pdf

caution is that often a healthcare leader, dealing with the gravity of day-to-day needs, can get so focused on the patient or situation in front of them that they may not realize the forces that are creating change and those that are potentially disruptive.

There is an exceptional book on the topic, *Upstream* by Dan Heath, that was actually inspired by a single parable ascribed to sociologist Irving Zola, using it in a public health context. You have likely heard it and if not, it's worth repeating. Heath shares, ***"We're always chasing emergencies, we're always putting out fires,"*** he said. ***"We respond after the bad thing has happened. And we so rarely make the time and devote the resources that we need to get upstream and solve these problems at their root."***

The Upstream Parable

(As shared by Dan Health at the
Alpha Summit by CFA Institute)

"You and a friend are having a picnic beside a river and you just laid out your picnic blanket. You're preparing to have a feast, when all of a sudden, you hear a shout from the direction of the river. You look back and there's a child thrashing around apparently drowning.

Instinctively, both you and the friend jump in and swim out to rescue the child. But after you bring the child safely back to shore and just as your pulse starts to return to normal, you hear another child call for help."

"So, back in you go," Heath said. "You fish out that child. No sooner have you done that, you hear two shouts. Now it's two kids in the river. And so begins this kind of revolving door of rescue."

"Just as exhaustion sets in," Heath said, "you notice your friend swimming back to shore, emerging from the water, and walking upriver."

"You say, 'Hey, where are you going? I can't do all this work by myself.' And your friend says, 'I'm going upstream to tackle the guy who's throwing all these kids in the river.'"

As we close this thought, the takeaway is this: it's not enough to simply recognize the pace of change — we must shape our days with intention so we can think clearly and address what matters most.

As we can all expect, technology is the juggernaut that is creating disruption all around us in so many incredibly powerful ways. I'm all for it and seeing the progress has been amazing to see firsthand. To think that innovation in technology is in the first "innings" is what keeps leaders wanting to stay in the game. Due to the many ways technology could be discussed, I am not going to dive into this in the book at any level of specificity. As well, I am going to avoid the Geopolitical and Climate topics that are covered in Accenture's report. We will cover the other three trends, including Talent, Economic and Consumer & Social as they relate to our industry.

- **Talent,** which includes indicators measuring the risk of labor shortages, level of employee engagement, wage costs and labor productivity, reflects the overall talent environment from a quantitative and qualitative perspective.

- **Economics,** which includes macroeconomic, financial and business indicators, reflects the overall economic disruption, financial volatility and business outlook.
- **Consumer & Social,** which includes indicators assessing social unrest and household savings, reflects the overall social climate as well as consumers' confidence in the future.

> **Pro Tip:** Before we move on to cover these topics, I will offer a pro tip on this grandiose topic of "CHANGE" (other than remembering to look upstream). If you find yourself struggling to stay current, which is likely, at the very minimum you should stay close to the consulting powerhouses such as Accenture, McKinsey and PricewaterhouseCoopers (PwC). They are stalwarts of the industry and have published consistent, exceptional research and analysis which can help you and your team tremendously. Most often they have annual or more frequent publications that identify macro trends and the headwinds and tailwinds we are likely to face in any given period. Flag this idea and put it to use. You will be glad you did!

Now, let's get started!

But first..., @timoelliot, a global innovation evangelist for Software as a Service (SaaS) offers some humor which may be just what we need to add some levity to the conversation.

For the final innovation exercise, the instructor asked everybody to practice pushing the envelope.

Let's Talk Talent

By now, you know that I am especially focused on the topic of talent. Here's what the Accenture Report says about talent:

> "The Index indicator analysis places Talent, **including issues such as skills shortages and lack of employee engagement**, just behind Technology as a top cause of change in 2023. Yet in the survey, C-suite leaders rank it fourth, behind Geopolitical and Consumer & Social. **This gap in perception underscores the importance for businesses of making their people a top investment priority** as they tap the potential of new technologies such as generative AI."[50]

We have talked about the power of the people and team and will be concluding the book on this essential topic. It is unfortunately far too common for leaders not to invest here as they should. I will say, I am a big fan of the work of the

50 https://www.accenture.com/content/dam/accenture/final/accenture-com/document-2/Accenture-Pulse-of-Change-2024-Index-Executive-Summary.pdf

Human Resource (HR) teams that are a key to many parts of "people management" for larger organizations.

I do want to be clear that I am speaking specifically to the manager's role in leading their teams and being an active and present champion for everyone they have the gift of leading. I do hope you will think about this part of your role as being a gift. When we partner with like-minded individuals hoping to make our world and healthcare systems the best they can be in any given moment, we all become better people and our community's win.

The report cites that 42% of C-suite leaders say skills shortage is one of the top 3 challenges that would hold back their organizations' ability to respond to change. It is particularly a major concern in the healthcare industry, with over half citing it. This is mission critical for the healthcare leader. We as leaders are faced with the realities of both labor and human capital needs as we aim to build strong teams. This is before we even get to ensuring we as an organization can excel in leadership and end up with cultures that thrive.

An article from the American Hospital Association covered some takeaways from a new study based on research conducted by the Mercer consultancy and its partner Lightcast. It projects changes to the U.S. healthcare labor market by 2028 by state and metro and micro statistical areas. [51]

The research goes into more detail, offering us thinking around three key areas:

---

51 https://www.aha.org/aha-center-health-innovation-market-scan/2024-09-10-5-health-care-workforce-shortage

1. **The growing shortage of healthcare workers in the United States** is caused both by a **decrease in supply and an increase in demand**. Increased demand is an inevitable reality of our aging population, which we have covered. Decreased supply is a more nuanced problem, and the report identifies three major factors underlying the observed decline:
    1. Covid-19 as a catalyst for the acceleration of resignations
    2. Ongoing burnout among healthcare workers
    3. Non-competitive compensation for some occupations
2. **Demands of an aging society** means higher costs. Healthcare expenditure data shows that older people understandably spend more money on services as they encounter more health issues. Associated increases in healthcare expenditure will thus continue to drive demand into the foreseeable future.
3. **The supply pressures unique to your part of the country** are important to know. The topic is nuanced, and I highly recommend diving into the report for solid data. It goes further into detail, covering which states are trending in a surplus or shortage. All in, you simply must understand what is going on in your specific region in order to manage it in the best possible way. You will also find here information on ancillary roles including Nursing Assistants and Nurse Practitioners.

So, what are we to do with this information? The primary goal for this read is for you to be incredibly aware of the diverging forces and begin to develop a personal and professional approach to the topic. The answers are as varied as there are leaders and organizations.

Aman Kumar Singh provides a strong thought as we wrap up this vast topic of talent:

> ***"In the relentless pursuit of excellence, the healthcare sector must embrace these innovative solutions, fostering a culture of continuous learning and development. As healthcare professionals embark on this transformative journey, the ultimate beneficiaries will be the patients, who will receive the highest quality care from a workforce empowered by cutting-edge knowledge and skills."*** [52]

As an aspiring or early career healthcare leader, your people must be top of mind and always at the top of the to-do list. This way, you will find your career to be not only successful, but also one that leaves a lasting impact on more lives than you can imagine.

Let's Confront Affordability

Did you know that the average premium for single coverage in 2023 is $8,435 per year and the average premium for family coverage is $23,968 per year? This is without including the cost of copays and out-of-pocket expenses that often exceed $5,000 if you have any type of hospitalization or are managing a chronic condition. It's easy to see why affordability is a major concern.[53]

---

52 https://www.linkedin.com/pulse/revolutionizing-healthcare-training-innovative-aman-kumar/

53 https://www.kff.org/report-section/ehbs-2023-section-1-cost-of-health-insurance/

The Pricewaterhouse Coopers (PwC) trend report, refers to the current (2024) period as the "Big Squeeze." I kind of like that and appreciate the clarity in the message. In my most recent healthcare role, our constant challenge and goal was delivering on affordability, access and experience. I suspect it will be our constant mission to conquer this over the next period for the United States. Is this sentiment true across all of healthcare?[54]

PwC's newest research on medical cost trends shares that Commercial healthcare spending growth is estimated to grow to its highest level in 13 years and is projecting an 8% year-on-year medical cost trend in 2025 for the Group market and 7.5% for the Individual market. "This near-record trend is driven by inflationary pressure, prescription drug spending and behavioral health utilization."[55]

So yes, I would say that the evidence demonstrates that all major parts of our system are impacted. Delivering on affordability will likely be a top trend for you to embrace and be prepared to address in your healthcare career.

PwC does offer guidance in their "Big Squeeze" report, suggesting that they believe there is **"a way out of compression for health systems and health plans."** Some of their ideas in broad categorization include:

- Affordability and Operations Strategies[56]
- AI and managed services at the point of reinvention

---

54 https://www.pwc.com/us/en/industries/health-industries/library/healthcare-trends.html

55 https://www.pwc.com/us/en/industries/health-industries/library/behind-the-numbers.html

56 You will often see organizations with an Affordability Council as a formal group to get after the multiple tactics required to conquer this beast. PwC even cites their own in the article.

- Digital delivery of technology
- Workforce transformation
- Deals to transform
- Customer advocacy and trust, reinforced by strong risk safeguards

Thankfully for us we will be using much of what we have been discussing to tackle these enormous challenges. We can look at the "Who is doing something cool" section to begin to see tremendous innovation when it comes to solving for better care at a better price. We will of course be locked into all things technology for years to come, and we will no doubt see mergers and acquisitions come together to create larger enterprises focusing on the big problems with greater pooled resources. We will see organizations such as Kaiser, and their new organization, Risant, begin to accelerate Value-Based Care. We may even see our nation's health systems be modified to address these great challenges. What will you be a part of in bringing forward solutions? Exciting to contemplate if you ask me.

Consumer and Social

As we have recently come through an election cycle and all the banter that comes along, it is clear that consumers don't know who or what to believe, and also that the opinions are often strong and founded in strong real-life stories and personal narratives. As long as I've been alive, a similar consumer opinion has been a part of the national conversation, and so I think it's fair to suggest that you will continue to see this as you go through your career, regardless of what party is overseeing the mechanics at any given time.

The Accenture report doesn't spend a lot of time covering details here, so I will take the approach here of focusing on consumer experience. As a healthcare leader, you will most certainly be met quickly with the concept of measuring consumer satisfaction, likely via the Net Promoter Score (NPS). The Net Promoter Score (NPS) is a widely used behavioral metric in the business world, measuring customer loyalty, satisfaction, and how likely someone is to recommend a company or brand. In healthcare, the information resulting from the process can unlock powerful insights into the relationship between patients and the brand of an organization. "The use of the NPS has evolved, as has the understanding that it's not the only metric needed for a comprehensive, well-rounded understanding of patients," says Press Ganey, a top player in the field.[57]

I'm glad to hear that. I personally am not the biggest fan of the overly simplified question that frames your overall score: *How likely are you to recommend Organization X to a friend or colleague?* I have seen so many answers here, including a patient saying, "I can't give you a good score, because I don't even live here, I was only visiting, so I can't recommend you..." That patient gave us a 0, tanking our averages. Ugh! I do, however, appreciate both the directional information it provides as well as the universal scoring that is helpful to size yourself up against your competitors. I will share that the questions asked after the primary NPS question provide rich information for leaders, and your organization makes the decisions as to what questions you want to ask, which can be powerful if they are designed well.

57 https://info.pressganey.com/press-ganey-blog-healthcare-experience-insights/unlocking-the-power-of-nps-in-healthcare

As you can see from the graph below, healthcare doesn't "win" in the category of NPS scores by industry. The average NPS score for healthcare falls between +38 and +58. This is where opportunity lies for all of us. It is my opinion that focusing on patient or consumer experience and delighting them should be our goal. I often read business books from other industries to discover ideas that may be brought over to healthcare.

One of my favorites is Danny Meyer's book, *Setting the Table***.** Danny is a world-famous restaurateur, and a guru in the hospitality world. His work is worth diving into. One of my favorite takeaways was: Imagine the power if everyone in the healthcare industry full-on served in that manner. **"Take every opportunity to exceed expectations."**[58]

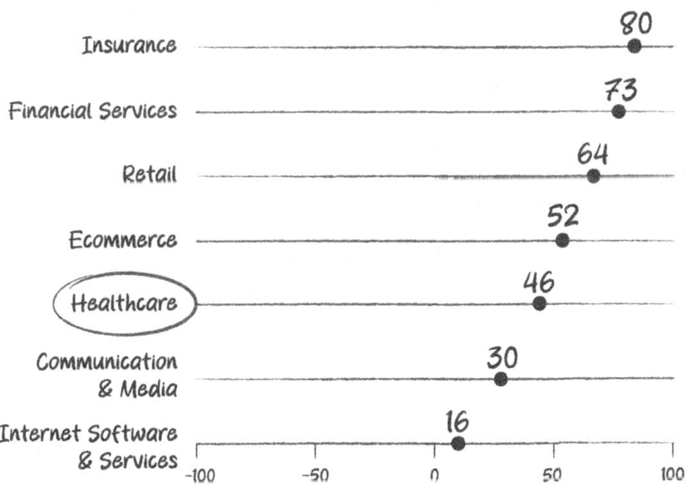

58 https://surveysparrow.com/blog/net-promoter-score-healthcare/

No matter what, the consumer/patient must always be prioritized. We have been given this incredible opportunity to make lives better for those we care for. I will end this section with a story about "Shirley." Shirley was a team member that worked on our launch team, and I immediately began to think of her as the "Chief Happiness Officer."

Shirley was pure magic and was able to bring light and hope to everyone she met, even to those where she didn't speak their language. (The universal language of a smile is perfection!) In this story, Shirley was exploring ways she could create a better experience for patients coming in for their visit. In addition to her front office role, she served on a small team charged with ensuring we were keeping health equity top of mind. She was the one who had the idea of creating a mini farmer's market in our lobby. She gathered some team members to support the mission, and within a week, we had fresh produce for our patients.

Now, some might say these patients didn't need it. What we experienced (to our surprise) was that many patients were grabbing a bag and filling it and thanking us profusely as they shared that they could no longer afford fresh fruit and vegetables post-Covid. Some took food for a shut-in neighbor or someone else in need. I love that beyond the smile, Shirley took action. In the simplest way, she created an experience that brought joy and impact to those in the community.

Let's all be more like Shirley and be the type of leaders to bring in more people just like her! It's my hunch that most team members want to bring about this type of love and care to those we serve.

The Big 3 (In Summary)

- **Change is here, it's inevitable and we must embrace it.**
- **The top three trends for us to watch (outside of tech) are Talent, Economics and the Consumer. Said otherwise, it's the People, the Money and the Patient.**
- **Be a Shirley, enable more Shirleys and continue to make healthcare better for our country, one community at a time.**

"A culture is strong when people work with each other, for each other. A culture is weak when people work against each other, for themselves."

—Simon Sinek

Chapter 11

Investing in Innovation and Transformation

"It is not the strongest of the species that survive, nor the most intelligent, but the one most responsive to change."

—Charles Darwin-known of his theory on evolution

The Price of Failing to Adapt

History is often a good place to look when thinking through what lies ahead. Whether it be Darwin's age-old quote *(circa 1800's)* or taking another look at the now famous Blockbuster demise story; a lot can be taken that is still undeniably true today. Blockbuster who at one time had over 9,000 stores, refused to adapt to a fast-moving industry. First, they continued to rely on the old business model of charging late fees. Second, they continued to invest in retail stores, seemingly ignoring consumer preferences that were changing to a more convenient online option. Finally, they had the chance to actually make a change by acquiring the tech innovator Netflix in the year 2000. They had many opportunities to adapt and continuously refused to see the changing landscape. In 2010 Blockbuster filed bankruptcy.

This is an attitude we never want to have in healthcare, as it has even bigger consequences. It's crucial to maintain the foresight needed to be a proactive healthcare leader.

Imagine yourself as a newly minted early career healthcare administrator. You are faced with the uncomfortable truth that revenue will not exceed costs this year. Along with that fact, some of your best team members have shared that they are being forced to take a second job at night to help pay the bills, realizing that their 2 to 3 percent annual increase is much lower than the rate at which the actual cost of living increases in their community. Your technology system is in desperate need of being upgraded, and the latest executive conference stressed that enhanced cyber-security investments should be made NOW. Your board wants you to consider the options on how the organization is going to survive another year. You came into this role excited and ready to create innovation and impact (not just survive). What are your choices?

This chapter will be focused on some of the potential solutions to this common challenge. At the most basic level, your goal will be to achieve it all. To be able to survive and even thrive in the midst of the incoming challenges. They are different in each time period in our country, but they have always been there, as this is a classic conundrum. The simple equation of matching revenue with expenses requires diligence, creativity and innovation. The great news is that there are now a few others interested in helping us arrive where we need to go. We will focus there, and specifically on how private equity and venture capital may be valuable strategic partners throughout your career.

Private Equity

One of my favorite organizations to learn from is the Aspen Ideas Festival, held annually during the summer in Aspen, Colorado. Thought leaders from across industries and the world come together to cover ideas and thought leadership about healthcare. It's truly inspiring, and while sometimes heady, it is worth the deep dive. One of those "rabbit hole" excursions found me listening in on the Aspen Ideas panel session titled, "Private Equity Pushes into Healthcare." In the session, Alex Azar, the 24th Health and Human Services (HHS) Secretary and an Adjunct Professor at the University of Miami Herbert Business School, shared the options that a healthcare leader may consider as they try to solve for the financial sustainability equation:[59]

1. **Self-funding (innovation)**
2. **Selling out**
3. **Going public if you can, although this is not generally possible in this situation**
4. **Debt financing**
5. **Exploring strategic partners with private equity**

Private equity (PE) has accelerated as an option in healthcare, and not only for the shiny and new technologies, but for medical practices in primary care, specialty care and even hospitals. The numbers are stunning. In 2021, PE firms poured more than $200 billion into the sector, compared to $41 billion in 2010. This reflects a 5X growth trajectory in a bit over a decade. Investors claim their capital will expand access to care, drive innovation, fund cutting-edge research,

59 https://www.aspenideas.org/

and create new jobs. This to me is promising, however, critics say that the interest in PE is driving further consolidation of the healthcare market, increasing costs, circumventing antitrust regulations, and threatening quality and oversight.[60]

So, how should we think about private equity? **In short, it can be described as an organization or person that is investing in a private company.** These are typically investments made in mature organizations, and their goal is to partner by offering their financial and consulting support in ways that help the group restructure or optimize in hopes of turning a substantial profit. The other key factor to understand is that PE deals take a shorter-term view. Their goal is typically to turn over a profit or strike a "deal" in no later than 7 years, with 3 being a more likely target. We can then know that if we do choose to engage with PE, we will likely be confronted with an intense plan to getting to success. (That is not to mean it should be avoided, but many physicians in my experience do not appreciate this fast-track approach.)

> **"Private equity is the intersection where ambition meets expertise, driving companies not just to evolve but to transform."**
>
> **—David M. Rubenstein, private equity pioneer, introduced by the Atlantic Council as a student of history, master analyst, and legendary philanthropist**

I wanted to provide some examples of PE activity that should be familiar. If they are not, it's worth looking up for a greater understanding.

60 https://www.aspenideas.org/sessions/private-equity-pushes-into-healthcare

- **The Optum acquisition of Change Healthcare (CHC) for $5.4B:** (In this case, Optum is serving as the PE investor.) The combined businesses share a vision for achieving a simpler, more intelligent and adaptive health system for patients, payers and care providers. Optum is focused on connecting and simplifying the core clinical, administrative and payment processes healthcare providers and payers depend on to serve patients. Their focus is on increasing efficiency and reducing friction, benefiting the entire health system, resulting in lower costs and a better experience for all stakeholders.[61]
- **Village MD acquisition of Summit Health/CityMD for $8.9B**: (In this case, VillageMD, Walgreens and Evernorth [Cigna] are serving as the PE investors.) The companies will have more than 680 provider locations in 26 markets. According to a news release from VillageMD, this combines "VillageMD's innovative platform and value-based care model with Summit Health-CityMD's expertise delivering multispecialty and connected care."
- **Humana's acquisition of Kindred Home Health in partnership with TPG Capital and Welsh, Carson, Anderson and Stowe (PE Companies named as the "Sponsors") for $800M:** (In this case, Humana has two PE partners which helped them complete the deal. Humana will own 40% and the Sponsors 60%.) This deal is a strong nod to the known need to create better solutions for our aging society in the ways of home health. The deal "advances Humana's integrated care delivery strategy to make it easier for members to engage in their health by

61 https://www.changehealthcare.com/optum

providing care to seniors living with chronic conditions in their home, a member preferred lower cost setting."[62]

There are truly so many examples, so I hope you will dig in here. The most important takeaway for you at this point is to understand that if you are involved in a seasoned organization, private equity is a resource that might help you achieve your strategic objectives.

Venture Capital (VC): The More Well Known Twin

Shark Tank has become one of America's favorite television shows since its inception in 2009. Shark Tank is based on private investors making bets as hopeful entrepreneurs share their stories and ask for support to achieve their dreams. Typically, there are not a lot of "healthcare orgs" as we think of them, but I did find one which was worth sharing below. It is one of the most successful ever in the history of the show. Who knows? Maybe healthcare consumer products will be the next focus for healthcare leaders. No doubt, they too need exceptional leaders who know the intricacies of the healthcare world.

Shark Tank Success Story

Founder and CEO Julie Cheek created Everlywell to offer at-home lab tests. Consumers can use the tests at home, and the collected samples are then shipped to partner laboratories. The results are reviewed by physicians and delivered digitally within days. Her goal was to make lab testing more affordable, accessible, and convenient to patients. Sound like a familiar goal? After appearing on Shark Tank, the company grew through partnerships with CVS and Target. Everlywell eventually acquired PWNHealth and Home Access Health Corporation, forming the parent company Everly Health.

---

62 https://humana.gcs-web.com/news-releases

- Shark: Lori Greiner offered a $1 million line of credit at 8% interest in exchange for a 5% stake
- Sales: $1.1 billion as of May 2023[63]

There is much more to VC than Shark Tank, but I wanted to get your mind firing on the topic. First, a couple of key points. One, you will often hear both PE and VC used interchangeably, which can get quite confusing, since they aren't the same thing. In short, VC should be considered a longer-term investment. It is often used to support startup founders as they hope to transform our world. For many, it is the sexier of these two investment options. You will see by the graph below the various stages from the seed round, advancing to round C, and sometimes beyond. Under that, you'll see the different types of venture capital.

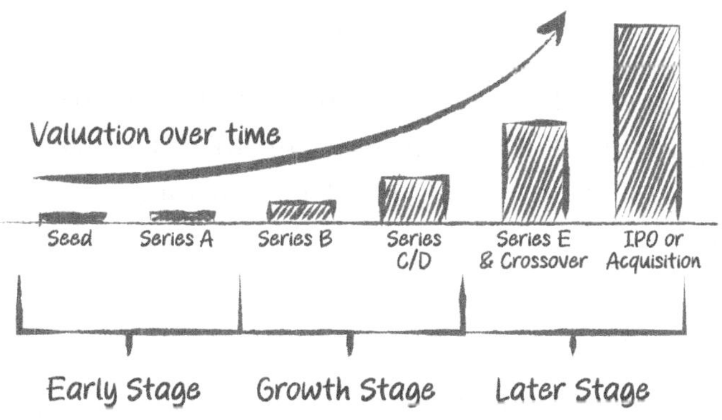

63 https://www.investopedia.com/articles/investing/082415/10-most-successful-products-shark-tank

Types of Venture Capital Funding

Seed stage

Seed stage funding refers to the first round of startup financing, typically pre-seed, seed, and angel rounds. VC firms tend to dedicate specialized funds for seed stage startups, with the hope of being an early investor in a unicorn.

Early stage

Early-stage funding refers to Series A or Series B funding rounds, which are usually done when a company has shown some traction and the potential to grow into a massive company.

Late stage

Late-stage funding refers to Series C and D rounds or further. At this stage a company is expected to go public soon or it might need the funds to expand into new markets.[64]

Now, I thought it would be helpful for you to meet some of the top digital health startup investors and their status as of 2024. More than likely there will be a few big winners.

---

64 https://www.investopedia.com/articles/personal-finance/102015/series-b-c-funding-what-it-all-means-and-how-it-works.asp

A Few Digital Health Startup Investors You Should Know

One of the top names in healthcare innovation and investing is JP Morgan. They are well respected and perhaps thought of as the premier organization to follow in this field. Their annual conference held each January in San Francisco is the flagship conference for healthcare investors and leaders. It is known as being both the largest and most informative healthcare investment symposium in the industry, connecting industry leaders, emerging fast-growth companies, innovative technology creators and members of the investment community. If you love innovation and ever get a chance to go, do it!

The origins of venture capital dates back to the 1940s. In the 1960s, it was still a cottage industry, but by the 1970s, that started to change. In the 1990s, the advent of the internet galvanized the industry, helped by notable venture-backed companies including Google, PayPal, eBay, Amazon, Netflix and Salesforce. The industry hit a setback toward the end of the decade as the dot-com bubble burst. This didn't put off investors for too long. Since then, the venture capital industry has matured into an established asset class, hitting peak investments of $350 billion in the U.S. in 2021 and $750 billion globally, as per PitchBook.[65]

Thanks to the researcher and author Ivelina Niftyhontas, we can take a snapshot in time and see who is leading the investment game as of 2024. Take a look:

65 https://www.jpmorgan.com/insights/investing/investment-strategy/what-is-venture-capital

The Top 3 VC Firms in the World[66]

1. Andreessen Horowitz

- Assets under management: $35 billion
- Investment to exit ratio: 16.71%
- Invests in: Startups of all stages
- Founded: 2009
- Location: Menlo Park, California

Andreessen Horowitz, also known as "a16z," is a relatively new player compared to some of the older venture firms. Marc Andreessen and Ben Horowitz founded Andreessen Horowitz in 2009. Both were already well-known tech entrepreneurs; Marc Andreessen as the co-founder of Netscape and Ben Horowitz, a co-founder alongside Andreessen, of the software company Opsware. a16z specializes in investing across various stages, from seed to late-stage ventures. It primarily focuses on healthcare, consumer, fintech, cryptocurrency, gaming, e-commerce, and cloud computing.

Notable investments include companies like Facebook, Groupon, Airbnb, Stripe, Twitter, Coinbase, Lyft, Function Health, Omada Health and Hippocratic Ai.

2. Sequoia Capital

- Assets under management: $85 billion
- Investment to exit ratio: 21.28%
- Invests in: Startups of all stages
- Founded: 1972
- Location: Menlo Park, California

66 Excerpt only. Full list found here: https://www.goingvc.com/post/top-10-vc-funds-whos-leading-the-investment-game-in-2024)

Sequoia Capital, arguably the most renowned VC firm, has a knack for attracting other investors when it takes the lead. Sequoia focuses on startups across various sectors, with a focus on the energy, finance, enterprise, healthcare, internet, and mobile sectors. The firm has a strong track record and actively assists a select group of founders in creating exceptional companies. Sequoia also manages investments for a small number of nonprofits like the Ford Foundation and the Boston Children's Hospital.

Notable investments include Apple, Cisco, NVIDIA, Google, Instagram, Linked In, PayPal, WhatsApp, and Zoom.

3. New Enterprise Associates (NEA)

- Assets under management: $25 billion
- Investment to exit ratio: 21.96%
- Invests in: Startups of all stages
- Founded: 1977
- Location: Chevy Chase, Maryland

New Enterprise Associates (NEA) is a U.S.-based venture capital firm founded by C. Richard (Dick) Kramlich, Chuck Newhall and Frank Bonsal. With nearly 50 years of experience, NEA remains a top choice for many startup founders. NEA invests globally in various companies; however, their core focus lies in the technology and healthcare sectors. Their diverse investment portfolio spans from seed funding to late-stage growth. NEA has a broad health-tech and biotech portfolio in numerous early and growth stage companies.

Notable investments include Patreon, Plaid, Upstart, Upwork, Onshape, and Uber.

Niftyhontas concludes her work:

> ***"As they seek out the next generation of unicorns and breakthrough innovations, their influence is set to endure, making them the guiding stars of the startup universe. The world of venture capital thrives on innovation, and these top firms are leading the way in the pursuit of tomorrow's success stories."***

> **Pro Tip:** The a16z podcast is excellent!

The great American dream is what VC is all about to me—or at least a big part of it. Understanding how transformation and innovation is funded (outside of in-house investments by organizations) is essential knowledge for a healthcare leader in today's environment. In fact, it is quite likely many of you will work with one of these firms or perhaps start your own on your journey.

Do They Bring *Enough* Value to the Table?

Before you start thinking too highly of these options, it is important to understand that both PE and VC have a shadow side—a dark side you must be aware of. Everything does, in fact, so asking ourselves tough questions is necessary. I briefly mentioned the fact above about the intensity of the process being a potential concern for physicians and their overworked teams. According to LinkedIn:

> ***"Critics argue that aggressive acquisitions and mergers by private equity firms can stifle competition, limit consumer choice, and entrench dominant market players, leading to higher prices, reduced innovation, and decreased economic dynamism."***[67]

---

67 https://www.linkedin.com/pulse/unveiling-veil-navigating-controversies-criticisms-2rbnf/

These are the top concerns, real factors to contemplate. Being clear about tradeoffs and expectations is essential for all involved. My greatest concern is the lack of true knowledge by members of the investment team. Can they REALLY help us if they don't know our nuances? Vinod Khosla, founder of Silicon Valley VC firm Khosla Ventures, and one of the most prolific investors of our time, pointed to my concern when he stated the following:

"Seventy to eighty percent of venture capitalists add negative value to startups."

He has continued to clarify his comment, which is now old by today's standards. In a Stanford Graduate School of Business address in 2015, he put his statement into perspective, contrasting the skills and experiences of VCs today with those who grew the industry in the 1970s:

"These guys earned the right to advise an entrepreneur," said Khosla, "because they fought the same battles in the trenches."

I add this due to the pace of the current environment. It is essential that you as a leader understand who is at the table and how they can and will help if we are to use this option. It may likely be well worth the risk in partnership. Assessing your organization's history, culture, and goals and ensuring alignment will be mission critical to achieve the shared goals of the possible partnership.[68]

68 https://thevcfactory.com/vc-value-add-vinod-khosla/

The Big 3 (In Summary)

- As a healthcare leader, you will be faced with the need to know your options in meeting financial goals and achieving organization strategies.
- Being well versed in both the PE and VC parts of healthcare financing will help you directly or indirectly. Indirectly, they are a terrific source of seeing where the trends are and what you can learn that might help advance your organization.
- It's still all about the people. No matter what strategic tactic you employ, aligning on skills, knowledge and culture is essential.

"The more intentional you are about your leadership growth, the greater your potential for becoming the leader you're capable of being. Never stop learning."

—John C. Maxwell

Chapter 12

Wellness: The Path to Our Future

"When you were born, you cried and the whole world rejoiced. Live your life in a way that when you die, you rejoice, and the whole world cries"

—Native American proverb

It is INVIGORATING to think about a healthier world! And I don't know about you, but since you are a healthcare leader or on the path to serving in that way, I imagine that you spend a lot of time thinking about HEALTH. After all, isn't that what we all want? Healthy communities? Healthy families? Healthy and vibrant lives? Even in sickness, a spirit of joy and hope?

We are going to spend our second to last chapter talking about the opposite of sick care as we know it. We are going to chat about the power of WELLNESS, specifically the overall wellness industry in the United States. When you think about the "future scan" for a healthcare leader, this to me is incredibly important and energizing. It is here I feel we can and will make a profound impact, and sooner rather than later.

I want to give you a bit of a primer on what composes the "wellness" industry. The Global Wellness Institute seems like a good place to start. It is the leading non-profit research organization for the wellness industry. They published new data (graph below) in April of 2024, sharing that the United States wellness industry is valued now at over $1.8T. That is incredible. To put it into some sort of context, the United States government has $1.46T budgeted for all of Social Security, which is the largest budget category according to treasury.gov.[69]

US Wellness Economy by Sector:

(Numbers refer to each market's global rank, growth from 2020-2022, and current market valuation.)

- Physical Activity: #1, +22.9%, $338.6B
- Personal Care & Beauty: #1, +13.4%, $310B
- Healthy Eating, Nutrition & Weight Loss: #1, +8.4%, $289B
- Wellness Tourism: #1, +31.8%, $259B
- Public Health, Prevention & Personalized Medicine: #1, -4.9%, $222B
- Wellness Real Estate: #1, +26%, $176B
- Mental Wellness: #1, +13.3%, $87B
- Traditional & Complementary Medicine: #2, +7.4%, $81.5B

69 https://fiscaldata.treasury.gov/americas-finance-guide/federal-spending.

- Spas: #1, +30.9%, $26B
- Workplace Wellness: #1, +8.1%, $18B
- Thermal/Mineral Springs: #6, +24.1%, $1.04B

Total Wellness Economy: #1, +14%, **$1.8T**

The report includes additional breakdowns on individual markets, such as:

- The physical activity sector, including:
    - Sports and Active Recreation ($67.2 billion)
    - Fitness ($41.3 billion)
    - Mindful Movement ($12.7 billion)
    - Fitness Tech ($17.5 billion)
- Healthy Eating, Nutrition, and Weight Loss
    - Healthy labeled food and beverages ($223.5 billion)
    - Vitamins and supplements ($49.9 billion)
    - Weight loss products and services ($20.0 billion)
- Mental Wellness
    - Self-improvement ($19.6 billion)
    - Meditation and mindfulness ($2.2 billion)
- US Spa Market
    - Hotel/resort spa ($6.5 billion)
    - Medical spa ($3.5 billion)[70]

70 https://globalwellnessinstitute.org/press-room/press-releases/united-states-wellness-economy-now-valued-at-1-8-trillion-the-largest-wellness-market-in-the-world/

I guess you could say that the American people are putting their health and wellness into their own hands, as rising healthcare costs are outpacing growth in the economy. There is definitely an interest in off-setting "sick care" in America, with our total Gross Domestic Product (GDP)[71] projected to climb to nearly 20 percent by 2032. [72]

I am going to lean into the categories that most touch the traditional healthcare leader, although there may be another full book to come on the many important conversations this data spurs on. We will be covering:

- **Food as Medicine (also known as Food Is Medicine, FAM or FIM)**
- **Digital health tools**
- **Holistic health (functional medicine, etc.)**

Food as Medicine: The Ultimate Prescription

Food as medicine, food is medicine, "let food be thy medicine"—the concept of applying evidence based nutritional science to care delivery.[73]

I love bringing something new to life that will make for a better healthcare ecosystem. Researching, designing and building is my go-to. The great news is that if you like that too, it doesn't matter if you are the guru of data, finance,

70 GDP is best described as the overall money spent in a given year on designated categories within the expenditure area; in this case, healthcare.

71 https://www.cms.gov/data-research/statistics-trends-and-reports/national-health-expenditure-data/nhe-fact-sheet

72 https://rockhealth.com/insights/an-apple-a-day-but-keep-the-doctor-in-play-a-primer-on-food-as-medicine-trends-solutions-and-business-models/

project management, marketing or compliance—there is a seat at the table for every skill. We have so much talent working on how to solve our sick care system. **Imagine what could be when that same talent is focused on HEALTH and PREVENTION.**

Let me start with a story I am super proud of. Not for me, but for the team I served most recently. We were charged with starting a care delivery organization from the ground up. We were beginning to work on the next phase of building out the clinical care model, and in my experience, one of the first actions you might take is to create a "Center of Excellence" (or CoE) approach that builds programs and pathways for patients related to specific disease categories—like diabetes or heart disease. I assumed we would follow suit in this situation. The data was clear that those would also be the best target areas for our population of patients. Our lead physician suggested that instead we start with a CoE around Lifestyle Medicine, to include Food as Medicine as a major focus. *(It is referred to as both "Food as" and "Food is," so pick your favorite!).*

Our team launched into building out a foundation to mitigate disease in the first place, and if disease is present, to help reduce its impact on the lives of our patients through lifestyle modification. It was refreshing to see the old script literally flipped. What a gift to be a part of that pivot.

Graph credit to The American Heart Association who have been an early major contributor to research and education in the Food as Medicine category.[74]

Also contributing to the Food as Medicine conversation in a significant way is the Rockefeller Foundation. In 1913, John D. Rockefeller established the Foundation to help our country solve humanity's toughest problems. The overall focus was to establish the whys and ease symptoms rather than alleviate with simple charity. In the words of Chinese philosopher Lao Tzu:

"Give a man a fish and you feed him for a day. Teach him how to fish and you feed him for a lifetime."

Food as Medicine impacts all demographic profiles; however, it is especially challenging for those in lower economic groups and under-resourced communities to have the needed access to both affordable and nutritious food. According to the Rockefeller Foundation, we experience a $1.1 trillion

73 https://www.ahajournals.org/doi/10.1161/CIR.0000000000001182

healthcare spend for diet-related diseases each year. This is equal to all the money we currently spend on food itself. Mind-blowing, really.

Food as Medicine programs can be as basic as a provider writing a prescription for healthy food and medically tailored meals. The idea of using food-based interventions to help prevent, manage, and treat diet-related diseases is simple, yet it has not been a part of the American known way of living.

"Integrating nutrition into our healthcare system would enable doctors to prescribe healthy food, reducing the need for invasive health services while lowering healthcare costs."

It's brilliant. This is one of the areas you will no doubt see traction on over the next several years. I'm so thankful for organizations like the American Heart Association, who I've spent over two decades of my professional career serving, and the Rockefeller Foundation for their support in making our country better. [75] [76]

These are some early positive learnings I thought would be helpful as well. As you can see, this is a hot topic—one we could easily spend the entire chapter on. I hope you will be inspired by these initiatives and get to know some of the companies or organizations driving progress in America's Food as Medicine journey.[77]

---

74 The Rockefeller Foundation and the American Heart Association have pledged $250 million to create a Food Is Medicine Research Initiative: https://www.nature.com/articles/s41591-023-02330-7

75 https://www.rockefellerfoundation.org/initiative/food-is-medicine/

76 https://tuftsfoodismedicine.org/wp-content/uploads/2023/09/Tufts-Food-is-Medicine-Institute_2023-FIM-Fact-Sheet.pdf

Digital Health Tools: Engaging the Patient in the Wellness Game

This area seemed particularly important due to both the progress we've made *(although we have yet to see the promises of the Jetsons—if you know you know!)* and what we can now see is truly possible in this powerful category. My professional viewpoint is that we have a lot of work to do in the category to bring the technology into the exam room. We are finding that while many have adopted smart watches and similar device trackers, their engagement in translating the data and partnering with their healthcare team to optimize their health isn't happening quite yet for most Americans. The healthcare system wasn't really built for this type of engagement anyway, which is why the new models of primary care are so important. Most provider offices don't have the extra time to spend analyzing this information on any given day to begin with.

When I have been a part of designing and building new care delivery organizations, we have discussed how to create pathways for engagement with digital health tools. What does it need to look like to be prepared to use patient digital health data during annual wellness visits? How can our teams best optimize internal processes and external/patient communication and engagement to encourage their best health?

With a primary care team as their "quarterback" and health champion, we learned early on that the consumer was not yet even close to being able to use these tools and the information they provide to get to their best health. There is hope shining on the horizon. Currently, Type 1 diabetics have become used to using continuous glucose monitors (CGMs) to track their insulin, and some elite fitness fanatics or the super curious early adopters are actively using devices for all manner of tracking, food, fitness, sleep, mindfulness, etc.

The truth is, we are still talking about the aches, pains and illnesses in the exam room most of the time. This is what we have become accustomed to. This is what we all hope to change and why this chapter is so important for future healthcare leaders.

Let's talk about the most obvious categories a bit more. But first, I do want to start at ground zero, and that is the Electronic Medical Record. This seems almost an odd topic to bring up, even to me, who helped launch one of the first EMRs, if not the first in the Kansas City market. Let's just say it's been around a while.

But here's what you should be prepared for as you launch: we haven't had the opportunity to optimize the power of the EMR. You can think of this like how we use our iPhone or any other newer device we have in our homes—there is simply so much that we don't use. We have spent the last two decades training providers to document electronically and to essentially "get the data in."

We haven't yet done much auditing to ensure there is accuracy and consistency among provider groups to ensure we can actually use this data for research and decision-making. As well, while most have figured out how to pull basic data for Patient Centered Medical Home or VBC quality metrics, many haven't been able to rebuild practice infrastructures to ensure providers have the necessary time to not only document, but to truly understand and use the data to have meaningful conversations and create strong action plans with their patients.

I am including this in order to find your starting place. The good news is that progress has been made, and there are new tools to layer on top of the EMRs, making extracting data and creating actionable recommendations much easier. I would suggest a simple framework or series of questions to help assess where your organization stands and in order to find out where the starting place is within your organization. This will help you determine the current value of your data and develop a solid roadmap for excellence. These are simple, and if asked in a truly curious manner, most all providers will be happy to engage in a frank conversation. We must first remember that they are scientists and went into medicine to truly help on the front lines. Objective data is essential for their understanding, processing, and engagement.

3 Simple Questions to Ask Each Provider

1. How confident are you are in the data the healthcare team puts into the EMR? Medications, Vaccinations, Patient Surgical and Health History, etc. (You can ask them to rate that confidence on a scale of 1 to 10, 10 being the highest.)
2. How confident are you that you have consistently and comprehensively included all you'd like to in your patient's medical record?
3. What are the possible gaps we might have today in our EMR data?

Now, we've briefly gotten EMR out of the way—or at least the aspect of it that directly affects the data digital health tools. Lets talk briefly about 4 known tools and the progress we have seen in each category.

Wearable Fitness Trackers

So much progress has been made here, with Apple, Garmin, Fitbit, and Whoop being the category kings and queens. The Oura Ring is also a major player. While some healthcare leaders believe this is ancillary to our roles, it is my belief that consumers over time will want a holistic viewpoint of their health, and the way they engage daily is often via these types of marketplace tools. We should remain aware, and it's fun to explore the progress and impact on health that these technologies create.

In a Harvard Health 2022 article titled, "Do fitness trackers really help people move more?", Julie Corliss went on a mission to find out if using a wearable actually has a measurable impact on activity level. According to the largest study to date on the topic, the answer is yes.[78] "Regular physical activity is vital for a healthy heart, and the improvements seen in this study could potentially make a difference," says Dr. Megan Wasfy, a cardiologist at the Cardiovascular Performance Laboratory at Harvard-affiliated Massachusetts General Hospital. The article adds:

> **"The increase in moderate-to-vigorous physical activity was close to 50 extra minutes per week, which is one-third of the 150 minutes recommended by the federal activity guidelines. The extra 1,200 daily steps taken when people were wearing**

78 See "Fitness trackers and activity levels: What's the evidence?"

trackers is about the same number that's been linked to a longer life in several studies. While 10,000 steps has been touted as a daily goal, research suggests that 8,000 steps a day is nearly as effective longevity-wise, particularly in older populations."[79]

I will say this is likely true. When I first had my Apple Watch, I experienced an increased motivation in physical activity. There are yet to be any long-term studies, and no doubt the industry will continue to track the potential progress. What we do know is that wearables help. With more engagement from the healthcare teams within the health systems, we will see greater success. I can honestly say that with just a bit of accountability from my healthcare provider, I would personally up my game. Raising our levels of attention and engagement to the power of the data is where I feel we will be next. In what ways could we use this tool to support our community health?

I do want to mention here a couple of opportunities which are low hanging fruit for the healthcare practice. One being the feature of heart rate monitoring, which can provide high and low heart rate notifications, irregular rhythm notifications, low cardio fitness notifications and even sleep apnea notifications. For many patients, this is a gamechanger. If it is a patient under the care of a parent or an older adult, when connected to others overseeing their care, this can be a lifesaving feature.

The Apple Watch integration with the Dexcom G7 continuous glucose monitor (CGM) has revolutionized diabetes management as well. With these models, users can view real-time blood sugar data directly on their wrist, eliminating the need for constant phone checks. We can only imagine this will

79 https://www.health.harvard.edu/heart-health/do-fitness-trackers-really-help-people-move-more

get better and better and new features will be added to support our health. As a leader, I like to consider how I can help support patients by integrating these technological advances into our healthcare operations. According to the Harvard article, only 20 percent of all Americans use a wearable tracker, which demonstrates that we have a lot of market share yet to engage!

Telehealth

This one hits me almost like the EMR category. It's surprising that it only just found its legs during the Covid-19 pandemic. Fortunately for all of us, it is finally here to stay. As I write this, our government and organizations nationwide are working through how we can best use all manner of "virtual" care to meet basic needs, support provider and care team shortages, and do a much better job of facilitating care for hard-to-reach populations (disabled, rural markets, etc.).

Major players include Teledoc, Amwell and key industry leaders such as Amazon Health. Many others are accelerating their efforts in the fast-moving space. There are too many to list and there is an entire category of virtual care "enablers" that help medical practices use their EMR and internal systems to conduct virtual care appointments. In my opinion, the best healthcare will be achieved when your own provider or care team has access to your medical records and can conduct the appointment, versus one that cannot see your history and key information.

The primary reason I wanted to include this topic is how important it is that we consider as leaders all of the channels we should have available to patients. Additionally, when addressing common dilemmas such as staffing shortfalls or patient engagement, it makes sense to understand in what ways we might optimize our telehealth platforms. Within my payer experience, I learned that many plans offer a basic virtual urgent care solution for members as a benefit. As a healthcare operations leader, I wasn't always aware of what services many health plans offer their members. (Often, they provide these services through outsourced partners such as Amwell to meet these needs for patients/members.)

In hindsight, I wish I had come out of my master's program with a comprehensive understanding of how payers think *(They want their members to have affordability and access!)* and how they often offer these types of tools in their health benefits packages. Knowing this can help us on the front-line better help patients navigate and experience care. We are all after the same goal, which is to get people to healthy. If they are sick, take care of that need. If they are well, keep them that way! Health systems, providers, payers—all of us together are better off knowing the nuances of the other providers and using the entire toolbox, if you will, in ensuring the best care process is in play![80]

Mobile Health Apps

Mobile Health Apps, like others in this category, are all about optimization and consumer engagement. It really is all about personalization when we get to this part of the conversation. We want to think about how we can get the patient to play a key role in their own health. It's the same story as above in terms of understanding that no matter where you work in the ecosystem of healthcare, our entire goal is healthier communities. Whatever we can do to make that happen, that is our North Star. I thought it might be fun to list some mobile health apps

---

80 A few to watch:

- https://www.teladochealth.com/
- https://amwell.com/landing.
- https://health.amazon.com/onemedical/urgent-virtual-care/

to, once again, get your mind firing on the possibilities. Perhaps you will design a mobile app that helps us move the needle!

Mobile Health Apps That Are Awesome!

Mental Wellbeing

- Headspace (mindfulness)
- Happify (positive Thinking)
- Breathe, Think, Do with Sesame (kids)

Fitness (Workout routines, tracking and coaching)

- Strava
- Nike Training Club
- Peloton

Nutrition (Track food intake, calories and manage dietary goals)

- My Fitness Pal
- Lose it
- Noom

Sleep (Analyze sleep patterns and offer soundscapes or guided relaxation to improve sleep quality)

- Sleep Cycle
- Calm
- Pzizz

Habit Tracking (Helps users build and maintain healthy habits, from drinking more water to exercising)

- Habitica (gamification)
- Streaks (iPhone)
- HabitNow (Android)

Remote Patient Monitoring (RPM) Tools

We are going to wrap up this section with a discussion on remote monitoring tools. So, what do we need to know or think about here? Remote monitoring is currently active in the continuous glucose monitoring space as well as becoming more popular with the smart scale tracking tools which provide weight and body composition data. Both examples are life-changing for those with chronic conditions. Imagine as a heart patient being able to see that you gained 10 pounds of water weight and your provider being able to see that critical information immediately and address a potential life-threatening health situation. Incredible.

According to a 2023 article from EMARKETER, providers using RPM-enabled home health monitoring systems and other telehealth delivery methods are already seeing reduced hospital readmissions. A win-win for the patient and the system. The University of Pittsburgh Medical Center, for example, reduced the risk of hospital readmissions by 76%, and held patient satisfaction scores over 90% by equipping patients with tablets and RPM equipment. Further, seniors are driving a positive return on investment from RPM technology and home-based care, largely due to the cohort's high incidence of multiple chronic diseases.

Where do we stand today as an industry? A KLAS Research report surveyed 25 healthcare organizations and found that 38% of healthcare organizations running RPM programs and focused on chronic care management reported reduced admissions, while 17% cited cost reductions.[81]

---

80 https://www.hcms.org/tmaimis/rpm

Insider Intelligence estimates 70.6 million US patients, or 26.2% of the population, will use RPM tools by 2025. All in, it's good information to know.[82]

We are at the kick-off, but the pace of the game will be fast, so we need to be ready.

Let's check out some organizations to watch:

- Dexcom Continuous Glucose Monitoring for Diabetics
- Honeywell Life Sciences time health monitoring system, which captures and records patients' vital signs both within the hospital setting and remotely.
- Medtronic Heart Monitoring

Holistic Health (Alternative/Integrative/ Functional Medicine)

> **"The power that made the body heals the body."**
>
> **— Shared by Dr. Michelle Robin, author and founder of Your Wellness Connection**

Back in the early 2000s I had a vision which included integrating Western medicine (commonly known as the US health system) and Eastern medicine (holistic modalities) into one initiative, "The Institute for Women's Health." We indeed launched it and it stayed active for a few years, but as I understand, it eventually fell victim to new priorities. The model had both traditional women's care with a premier OB/GYN group leader and founder and also included integrated breast health, urology, chiropractic, massage, clinical research and more. We had a small but beautiful lecture hall designed and built as we knew

81 https://remetrichealth.com/improving-patient-retention-with-remote-patient-monitoring/

education had to be a centerpiece. It was beautiful and I'd love to resurrect the idea all over this country.

> **Fun Fact:** Dr. Michelle Robin, who I quote above, was a founding member of The Institute for Women's Health initiative in Leawood, Kansas. She has continued to amplify wellness across the country, and has authored multiple wellness books and has a podcast you should check out, "Small Changes, Big Shifts."

The goal for this chapter is for healthcare leaders to understand that there is something more than the typical care we see in our country's traditional health system. The idea of integrative or alternative medicine can be challenging topics; they are broad and can easily become confusing to providers and consumers alike. How do we know what to pay attention to? In the scope of competing priorities for healthcare leaders, they can be in the back seat for most. So, how does it fit in and how should we move forward in this space? How can holistic or wellness modalities help us solve for our greatest challenges? How can we integrate services and ensure we remain evidence-based?

Regardless of how we answer these questions, we need to know the facts. An April 2024 study shares that almost 1 out of every 4 Americans use some type of alternative medicine or treatments when confronting their own health. This includes everything from using supplements to supporting their health by seeking support from chiropractic physicians or acupuncture practitioners.[83]

Additional core facts (below) via a 2022 Harvard article support the thinking that we should stay close to this and do what we can

82 https://www.statista.com/statistics/1341758/us-adults-who-used-select-alternative-medicine-treatments/.

to both be educated and prepared to lead in this area. If you read in between the lines, you will quickly be able to decipher that while the older generations may not be the most avid users, the generations coming up indeed are very open-minded to doing all they can to maintain a life of health and wellness. They are looking to alternatives to our traditional systems of care. I expect this category to grow tremendously during the next several years. Are you ready? (Another fun topic if you ask me!)

Alternative Medicine Stats

"Two-thirds of Americans ages 50 to 80 uses at least one form of integrative medicine — to boost health or mood. **But fewer than one-fifth have talked to their doctor about doing so, a new survey suggests.**

The findings, derived from the University of Michigan National Poll on Healthy Aging, also indicate that 92% of respondents considered integrative medicine strategies to be 'very' or 'somewhat' beneficial.

Women were more likely to use the techniques than men, as were midlife adults (ages 50 to 64) compared with older adults (ages 65 to 80).

Researchers surveyed 2,277 people ages 50 to 80 online and by phone in January and February 2022. Respondents said they had used integrative approaches to treat or prevent pain, insomnia, and digestive problems or to address a severe physical injury. They reported also using these techniques to relax, manage stress, or improve mental health issues such as anxiety or depression."[84]

83 https://www.health.harvard.edu/staying-healthy/us-adults-like-integrative-medicine-but-few-discuss-it-with-their-doctors

Another key part of this conversation is life expectancy. What could drive more emphasis in this area? To me, the logical part of this is that we are living longer lives on average. Although there is controversary about a possible recent drop in life expectancy, the truth is that life expectancy has risen in the United States for many years. It was 47 years in 1900, 68 years in 1950, and 79 in 2019 according to a Harvard 2022 study.[85]

Macrotrends.com suggests that it remains around 79 and will likely continue to rise. The one thing I know for sure is Americans are going down fighting. Last year alone, I read three newly published books on the topic:

- *Outlive* by Peter Attia, MD
- *Life Force* by Tony Robbins, with Peter Diamandis, MD, and Robert Hariri, MD, PHD
- *Young Forever* by Mark Hyman, MD[86]

When we think of overall health and wellness and then consider the massive healthcare ecosystem and our chosen field, we begin to see just how much work there is to do. All of it wrapped into one beautiful picture that is our health—our one life and those we ultimately serve. As we move into the final chapter, let's keep this fresh in our minds.

Imagine your loved ones and community living a healthy life full of vibrancy and joy. Free time filled with walks in nature and a healthy dose of sunshine, and perhaps a bit of dancing. Mindfulness and gratitude… inhaling all of the good and exhaling what is not helpful.

86 https://www.health.harvard.edu/

87 https://www.macrotrends.net

Having access to amazingly nutritious meals that heal upon arrival...colorful, flavorful, created with love. Plentiful hydration that refreshes the entire body by the hour. Days of healthy movement and playlists that bring the soul to life. Warm relationships that are packed with support and meaning —and lots of laughter!

And finally, an abundance mindset, driven by purpose and a deep spiritual knowing of the impact one can make. Now that is a life I'd love to live. How about you?

Measuring Healthy Days

The last thing I want to mention is how the CDC measures the population's health-related quality of life. They propose asking the following questions of the patient:

- *Would you say that in general your health is excellent, very good, good, fair or poor?*
- *Now thinking about your physical health, which includes physical illness and injury, how many days during the past 30 days was your physical health not good?*
- *Now thinking about your mental health, which includes stress, depression, and problems with emotions, how many days during the past 30 days was your mental health not good?*
- *During the past 30 days, approximately how many days did poor physical or mental health keep you from doing your usual activities, such as self-care, work, or recreation?*[87]

I have personally worked with this process to assess how members are feeling in their lives. All in, the Healthy Days metric provides a good indicator that we should consider using more broadly in understanding the true "wellness" of our patients.

---

88 https://archive.cdc.gov/www_cdc_gov/hrqol/methods.htm

As we progress to our final chapter, it will be clear that the critical lever to all of this is exceptional healthcare leaders. This includes both clinical and non-clinical. They must be able to help our healthcare organizations, neighborhoods, communities, states, and country not only navigate sometimes rocky waters, but also to achieve the ultimate goal of our best health. Again, I am so glad you are here. If you are in this far, you are officially on the mission with us. The world is counting on you to embrace healthcare with your heart, soul and mind.

The Big 3 (In Summary)

- **The path to our future in this country will be forged in a universal focus on both Health and Wellness, with Lifestyle Medicine, including Food as Medicine, as a central part of the success of achieving our best health.**
- **Healthcare leaders will need to create and design integrations with all manner of technology including remote health monitoring into the day-to-day practice and health system operations.**
- **The healthcare ecosystem will continue to expand in the area of all things Alternative and Integrative Care. As our society ages and life expectancy expands, we will see much focus on the use of these modalities to create more "healthy days."[88]**

---

88 Healthy day calculations were introduced by the Center for Disease Control and Prevention (CDC) in 1993 to help measure how the population is feeling about their health. Healthy days are the positive complementary form of unhealthy days. Healthy days estimate the number of recent days a person's physical and mental health was **good** (or better) and is calculated by subtracting the number of unhealthy days from 30 days.

"EXCELLENCE IS THE NEXT FIVE MINUTES

Excellence is NOT an aspiration.

Excellence is NOT a hill to climb.

Excellence is the ultimate short-term strategy.

Excellence is the next five minutes.

Excellence is your next ten-line email
— or 25-word text.

Excellence is the first three minutes of
your next meeting.

Excellence is listening . . . really really ("fiercely,"
"aggressively") l-i-s-t-e-n-i-n-g.

Excellence is sending flowers to the hospital where
your top customer's Mom is having major surgery.

Excellence is going out of your way to say "Thank
you" for something "small."

Excellence is pulling out all the stops at warp
speed to respond to a "minor" screw-up.

Excellence is adding a final touch to a final touch
to a final touch.

Excellence is the next five minutes.

(Or it is nothing at all.)"

—Tom Peters

Chapter 13

The Grand Finale: Exceptional Leadership

"Never doubt that a small group of thoughtful, committed citizens can change the world; indeed, it's the only thing that ever has."

—Margaret Mead, American anthropologist

I am so thankful to be at this point in the journey of writing this little book. We have covered many roads over the past twelve chapters and many complex issues that have taken me through many hills, some mountains and lots of valleys over my 25+ year career in healthcare. When I left my first larger role as CEO of Kansas City Internal Medicine (shout out to our exceptional team!), they gave me an engraved crystal bowl with the above quote on it. I always had this posted somewhere in my office, often in strategic decks, business plans and any way I could make it front and center.

I'm not sure why this quote has always deeply resonated with me. I suppose that at the spirit level, I know that together we can indeed leave our world better than we found it. All generations are given their own set of challenges to address and victories to celebrate. Our country has moved at such an incredible pace. With new technologies every day, we can expect to outpace every other generation. Now is your time to shine and thoughtfully bring forward continuous improvement and progress.

I will end this book where I started, which is with honoring PEOPLE.

Without exception, this is truly the only leadership skill that will ensure both your success and personal happiness. I'll be honest, leading people is gritty work. It is caring when you don't want to. It is doing mental acrobatics to try to understand their perspective. It is endless conversations, many of them requiring great courage (and pain). It's just plain hard.

There is also no greater joy in the workplace than seeing someone that only you believed in succeed, in being a part of a team that achieves great outcomes, in watching a patient's journey go from what they thought might be the end to true health and happiness. The rewards, my friend, are endless.

The Results are Powerful

I want you to imagine right now that you are the leader of a growing healthcare organization. Your team spends endless hours in direct patient care, and in work groups trying to solve for the needs of their population's health. Your team members are all unified and committed to truly creating a special experience for their patients and getting them to health. You each are tired, but you forge ahead each day hopeful.

It's a typical Thursday, and in morning huddle, the lead provider shares that Mr. Williams will be in today. She shares that he has been working closely with the Medical Assistant, Behavioral Health team, and Care Coach to get his A1C in check, finally losing some weight, which had been a life-long challenge, and getting his mental wellness game on a better path. It's been a struggle, and in fact, recently he had shared that he had a plan to end his life.

The clinical team looks up his latest lab results and sees the incredible news that his latest numbers have him hitting his goal. The Behavioral Health leader shares that he is also making progress on his mental wellness and has shared how happy and lighter he feels. The Medical Assistant shares that she has talked to him 3 times since his last visit and he is cautiously optimistic, but sometimes distressed. She has continued to encourage him and be a personal champion of sorts.

Later that day, you are in your office and hear what sounds like a celebration out in the lobby. To your delight, you see that your team has taken it upon themselves to create a red carpet experience and a mini-parade cheer line to celebrate his victory. (They received his permission first, of course!) All you can do is think, "WOW! That is teamwork in action." That, my friends, is a VICTORY STORY in so many ways. Everyone won that day—especially the care team.

This is actually a real story. This kind of success is what you live for as a leader. It's a direct result of the entire leadership team being unified on shared goals of communicating well with one another and literally changing lives.

In the rest of the chapter, I am going to offer you a few concepts I believe will help you also **create a strong culture of excellence.**

A Culture of Excellence is:

- A differentiator
- Who we strive to be
- The collective personality of our organization
- Results in action
- Always a work in progress.

Let's Talk About Culture

I have often asked my team, and I encourage you to do the same, how they define culture. In a roundtable discussion with a group of new team members, there are always many answers.

"It's the power of the team."

"It's the day-to-day environment."

"It's something you can only feel."

It's a great discussion, and especially interesting when they share that no one has ever even asked them, nor did their prior work experience include any type of focused onboarding effort (or at least an obvious one) on the topic.

You have likely heard the famous Peter Drucker quote, "Culture eats strategy for breakfast." It should be engraved in every new leader's mind from my point of view. Without a positive culture, we don't even get to breakfast. We can create all manner of strategic tactics and big plans, bring forward innovative ideas and consider major investments that will make our businesses thrive, but if we don't first lock in the people side of the equation, we will most likely fail in our ability to execute.

Culture Stats from Forbes

- When we're happy, we work harder. The Department of Economics at the University of Warwick found that satisfied employees are a whopping 12% more productive than the average worker. When employees feel valued and supported, they are more likely to be motivated and give their best effort. This translates to improved efficiency, innovation and overall performance.
- A remarkable 88% of job seekers consider a healthy work culture vital for success.
- The impact of company culture on revenue is undeniable. According to Gallup, companies that prioritize culture experience a significant 33% increase in revenue. Here, the role of skilled managers cannot be underestimated, as they contribute to 27% of this revenue growth. Effective leadership fosters a positive work environment, inspiring employees to excel and achieve outstanding results.[89]

89 https://www.forbes.com/councils/forbesfinancecouncil/2023/09/14/building-a-company-culture-to-drive-success/

People over Process

I will likely be writing an entire book on this concept. Honestly, it's my calling card as a leader. Often, I'll have a child-like drawing on my whiteboard which pretty much makes this clear: when serving our teams, we need to ALWAYS consider the people side of things first.

I remember clearly when this began to take form in my mind. It was in the early, but not too early, (2008 approximately) days of my healthcare executive level career. I had one of my leadership team members in my office, and she was offering her passionate plea for us to create a policy addressing team members who were late to work. She had done her homework and gotten some of her peers on the leadership team to support her idea.

Now, I know this seems easy at first glance, but once I looked at the facts, I saw that the strong majority (like 97%) were not only on time or early, but actually worked many extra hours on behalf of our patients. I believe the month before we had even conquered the overtime policy in our management meeting. We did not have a problem, in other words, with team members being late...What we had were a few bad apples so to speak. We ended up having a "healthy" conversation about how I felt her solution lacked leadership. To me, this was trying to solve a leadership challenge with management 101. I wrote some sort of memo to the leadership team, and I sure wish I could find it. It was something with a header like, "The Leadership Crutch."

The message of the memo was that we can't solve what ought to be a simple conversation that a manager needs to have with a problem employee with a policy that impacts the entire office. That's not fair, and it lacks courage. She ended up truly appreciating the conversation and embracing the leadership approach. (I'd like to insert here that I don't always get it right, but in this case, we *all* agreed that we needed to take a step back.)

Process refers to everything we do in the organization. The People over Process concept is to remind us that with every single one of those important processes, how they impact the people needs to be considered:

1. How will this process impact the team? Who is involved? Who needs to be communicated to?
2. What could go wrong? What did we not consider?
3. How can we make it even better than the draft we are looking at? Does it have any unintended consequences?

I will throw a word of caution here by sharing that you have to be super clear that you are not suggesting that process isn't important. Similar to the airline industry, the healthcare industry needs a lot of strong processes. Strong processes ensure we are providing exceptional healthcare—following standards, crossing every *t* and dotting every *i* that is essential. As with everything in communication and leadership, giving the proper context and ensuring team understanding and alignment is needed.

Now, I want to drive home the point that we can't take care of our external patients if we don't take care of our internal team FIRST.

People First

I looked through my archives and found that this is how I typically size up this concept in my own "Culture Decks."

PEOPLE FIRST

- No titles, just positions focused on individual & team excellence.
- We hire top talent, who desire to achieve great & meaningful work for our city and neighborhoods.
- We collectively own the outcomes and strive onward.
- We encourage trust, integrity and authenticity.

Culture deck excerpt

What this is saying is that each and every day, we have to ensure our team has what they need so that in turn, they can take care of their patients and/or others in the organization they serve. One of the most common complaints I have received about managers is that they don't follow up on what the team members need. It is often super easy. I even had a team member last year that didn't have a stapler or pen on their desk when they joined. After asking for over two weeks, they shared the story with me. Of course, that is a rare example, but it's stated so you can see how simple things can get in the way. When we don't follow up as leaders, the team feels uncared for and that eventually rolls into their performance.

When you start out the day with your morning huddle, check in on the team. Even a visual check will do. *Is everyone smiling? Energy levels good? Anything I as the leader should be aware of?* There will be plenty of times when someone has had a tough morning be it traffic, not feeling great or an unexpected home situation. Sometimes it's more serious, but typically not. One way to take care of your team is to provide a safe space and let everyone know upfront that if that is them, to simply let you know and if they need, they can step out.

Teams thrive on positive energy. Giving someone a bit of room while allowing the show to go on is just plain being a good human. We have to take care of each other. As you peruse the quotes at the end of the chapter, they will add strength to this message. We all have *days*, and if we are to thrive in a workplace, knowing our team has our back makes all of the difference.

Seat at the Table

This one to me is the essence of community. We have this great opportunity to serve, and if your culture can establish a philosophy of everyone having a seat at the table, you will be better for it. I've seen it firsthand on so many occasions, I could never count them all. The essence of this is ensuring that the team is focused on serving well, by serving each other and the community. We all know that many personalities make up any group. This is no different. It's important to include this in your Healthy 1:1s, that we discussed earlier.

I recommend one each month for basic business ("How's it going? How are you? How can I support you?") and covering any work issues that need to be addressed; and then one each month for development reasons only ("What are your goals and how can I support you in those?").

Engaging team members by finding out what gets them excited is the goal. In the example about "Shirley," she was motivated to help serve the community by providing food they may not be able to otherwise get. Some team members will want to be on a population health team, some on data-focused teams, and some will want to serve the organization out in the community. I do like to stress that leaders who hope to continue to grow in their career should all serve on a community board in some capacity.

This could look like representing the organization at the monthly Chamber of Commerce events or serving on a non-profit board which interests them. As a leader, you are creating something that has a higher purpose, and people in general want to be a part of something bigger than themselves. As the African Proverb goes, "If you want to go fast, go alone. If you want to go far, go together."

I have seen healthcare organizations bring entire communities along, and improve their brand reputation at the same time, by participating in community walks, such as the American

Heart Association Heart Walk, The Susan G. Komen Breast Cancer Walk and the Bike MS ride to support multiple sclerosis. Honestly, there are so many, and community organizations make a huge impact for themselves as well as the cause when they support these events as a team.

There is something so invigorating when you see 100 of your team members, their families and pets show up on a Saturday morning to support a meaningful cause. The bonding alone and the joint feeling of pride is tremendous. Encourage your team members to have a seat at the table and get involved by joining your entire team as you work together to build a stronger team and a healthier community.

Final Thoughts

At my high school, we had to meet with the counselor one or two times a year to go over our class schedule, check in on how we were doing, etc. I have looked back often and thought of how powerful it would be for all of us to have a similar check-in at least once a year, a sort of "life coaching" session, where we could cover all of the basic wellness categories. Even better if that was with our primary care team leading the conversation. Something far more holistic focused than the typical annual wellness visit. Perhaps we will see this model soon!

My great hope is that you have been able to find in this book a few "gold nuggets" to take along with you on your journey. Being an exceptional healthcare leader starts and stops with the PEOPLE. My best wishes to you as you adventure into creating a healthier world for all of us!

The Big 3 (In Summary)

- It's truly all about the people.
- Culture does indeed "eat strategy for breakfast."
- Three "must-have" principles to live by as a healthcare leader:
    1. People over Process
    2. People First (internal and then external)
    3. Seat at the Table (build a team engaged both within the organization and the community)

ACKNOWLEDGEMENTS & THANK YOU

Writing this book has been shaped by the people who have walked alongside me in my career and my life.

First, my deepest gratitude goes to my family. Your steadfast support, patience, and understanding through years of dinner meetings, late nights, early flights, and countless calls have been the foundation that allowed me to grow as a leader. Your belief in me has fueled my belief in the work.

To the extraordinary teams I've had the privilege of working with—thank you for showing me, time and again, what it means to serve with excellence. You have collectively impacted hundreds of thousands of lives with the passion and care you bring to this world. What an honor to be a small part of that impact!

At Kansas City Internal Medicine, I learned so many things, but what stands out is the absolute power of a unified team. Your commitment to both clinical quality and human connection set a standard I've carried throughout my career.

To the CenterWell Senior Primary Care team at Humana—thank you for your passion in building care models that respect the dignity and individuality of every senior. You reminded me daily that leadership in healthcare is, at its core, an act of service.

And to the Prosano Health launch team at Blue Cross and Blue Shield of Arizona—what a privilege it has been to help shape something bold and new. Your courage to innovate, your dedication to doing the right thing for members, and your unwavering collaboration inspired this book more than you know.

This work is a reflection of the many lessons I've learned from you all. It is my hope that the ideas within these pages will serve leaders—present and future—as well as you have served me.

My best always, Lori

Made in the USA
Coppell, TX
20 January 2026

68760299R00115